Media Magic:
Profit and Promote with Free Media Promotion

Marisa D'Vari

"Marisa presents useful, inexpensive, easy-to-follow steps for publishers seeking media attention in an energetic, breezy and upbeat style. A fun read, as well as presenting practical info."

Jan Nathan, Executive Director
Publisher's Marketing Association (PMA)

"D'Vari teaches you insider tricks for mastering PR and creating a media feeding frenzy. Follow her advice and reap the rewards."

Marilyn Ross, author, *Shameless Marketing for Brazen Hussies* & *Jump Start Your Book Sales*

"On-the-air book promotion is free but you must get booked and you must perform. Marisa shares her wealth of experience and tells you how to get on and how to be a star. Marisa's book is concise, direct and to-the-point. It provides valuable answers, tips and guidance without wasting your time.

Dan Poynter, author, *The Self-Publisher's Manual*

"Could getting airtime on radio and TV really be as easy as Marisa D'Vari makes it seem? Based on her experience as well as those of others who know the inside story on broadcast exposure, the book offers solid advice, techniques, and encouragement in a clear and organized presentation. D'Vari provides the formula, facts, and foundation to help anyone get on radio and TV and perform successfully. If you want to leverage these far-reaching media channels, this book will help you do it like a pro."

Mary Westheimer, CEO BookZone

"Read Marisa's book. Internalize its wisdom. Implement just twenty percent of it, and you'll be ahead of ninety percent of everyone else on the interview circuit. Do yourself a favor and give yourself a head start with this material."

Gregory J.P. Godek, author of the 1.7-million-copy bestseller *1001 Ways To Be Romantic*

"I spent the better part of a year looking for a secret entrance to media success for my first book. Had Marisa's book been available, I would have been a celebrity sooner and sold a lot more books. Marisa is like a master magician revealing her secrets. Regardless of what you've written, you need to read this excellent guide to media success."

John Fuhrman, author of the International bestseller, *Reject Me, I Love It!*

"For its marketing exercises alone, Marisa's book is a pragmatic, must-read for writers who plan on promoting their work through the media."

Mark Levy, author, *Accidental Genius: Revolutionize Your Thinking Through Private Writing*

"Marisa's book is the quintessential guide to turning yourself into a media star guest. Marisa D'Vari shares her insider's expertise and secrets to help you conceive and carry out effective media plans for any objective — without needing a huge budget. Publicity is the name of the game in success, and her publicity course will make you a winner!"

Rosemary Ellen Guiley, PhD, author, *Breakthrough Intuition*

"Marisa is one unstoppable powerhouse promoter! She's a highly motivated self-starter, unwilling to take "no" for an answer. Her advice will be a welcome kick in the pants for anyone stuck with ideas on how to promote their book or product."

Michael Wiese, President MWP Productions

"It's no secret that getting on TV is one of the quickest routes to boost book sales. The mystery is how to get on. As a TV host, Marisa knows the secret. I'm just amazed she's willing to share but she does just that in her lectures and her book."

Melba Newsome VP of Publications for the American Society of Journalists and Authors (ASJA)

"As anyone who has appeared on her talk show can attest, Marisa D'Vari is always meticulously prepared on the details but oriented toward the big picture. The beauty of her book is that she teaches you as a guest exactly how to maximize your advantage while appearing through any broadcast media. Using the picturable term 'MAGIC' both in its literal and acronymic contexts, Marisa provides an understandable — and, more importantly, a RE-memorable—series of suggestions that will advance whatever projects you're promoting. A truly helpful, nuts-and-bolts guide to spreading YOUR word."

Jeremiah Healy, author of the crime novels *Spiral and The Only Good Lawyer*

"Even with my 50-plus years as a professional in the PR field, I learned a lot of new things from this book, proving that you *can* teach an old dog *new* tricks!" **From Irwin Zucker,** Founder/President Emeritus Book Publicists of Southern California

"Become an instant insider on the media circuit ... D'Vari debunks all the myths that becoming a 'great guest' for radio or TV is difficult by sharing her personal insights and how to's so anyone can make media magic!" **Tracy Day,** Principal t.b.d. Publicity

"Marisa speaks here with experience and savvy. Follow her advice and you'll get your fifteen-plus minutes in the media spotlight!" **Marcia Yudkin,** author, *Six Steps to Free Publicity* and 9 other books

Published 2002
DEG International Publishing
220 Boylston Street
Boston, MA 02116
Email publisher@deg.com
http://www.deg.com
(617) 451-9914

Cover Design by Nikki Kramer
Interior Layout by Jason Sands

Although the author and publisher have made every
effort to ensure the accuracy and completeness of
information contained in this book, we assume no
responsibility for errors, inaccuracies, omissions, or any
inconsistency herein. Any slights of people, places, or
organizations are unintentional. This book is not
intended to offer legal or financial expert advice.

DEDICATION

For sheer brilliance, Ron D'Vari is already far ahead of the crowd.

Outrageous good looks, sophistication, and elegance stack the cards heavily in his favor.

Thanks, Ron, for shinning your light and magic on this book!

WITH APPRECIATION ...

Thanks Julie Child, Robert Mondavi, Alan Dershowitz, Charlie Palmer, Todd English, Daniel Boulud, Adam Tihany, and all the other guests who have appeared on my TV show for making the magic!

Tracy Day and Marcia Yudkin, Marilyn Ross and Jan Nathan, Dan Poynter and John Kremer, much appreciation for your inspiration.

Lloyd, Janet, Bill - wow, what a dream team!

Ron, kudos for being such a powerful magician and crafting such magnificent manifestations. L.V.X.

Presentation Skills
and
Media Training

Do you realize that over 95% of the message revealed in your presentation is non-verbal?

That your audience and clients react more strongly to your *unconscious* body language than the words that come out of your mouth?

Discover the *excitement* of motivating clients and employees to action, positioning yourself as a leader in your field, and closing more deals with Marisa's Magic!

Marisa D'Vari works with clients in corporate training sessions to strengthen the company's overall image and efficacy of its executives. She also works with private clients to enhance their professional image in the media and their industry.
Contact her at mdvari@deg.com or visit her web site, http://www.deg.com.

About the Author

Marisa D'Vari
Speaker ▲ Author ▲ Consultant

Marisa D'Vari began her career as an entertainment industry executive in California before launching the syndicated television show, *A Taste of Luxury*.

Now based in New England, she is the president of DEG Communications, which gives executives and entrepreneurs effective presentation skills and media training.

D'Vari has been seen in London's *Financial Times*, *Ritz-Carlton Magazine*, *Robb Report*, and other prestigious publications.

Preface

Hi! Welcome to the *exciting* world of the media.

Please consider me your coach and muse, introducing you to creative marketing and promotional techniques to increase visibility and profits.

I'll be here every step of the way to help you:

☑ Outline your media goals

☑ Target the right media for your objective

☑ Identify and contact TV and radio show producers

☑ Put the right "spin" on your message

☑ Add magic to your media release

☑ Craft a knock-'em-dead pitch letter

☑ Master the elements of a winning media kit

☑ Zap on-air jitters

And much more!

TABLE OF CONTENTS

Introduction

The Magic of Free Radio and TV Promotion

Me?! on *TV?!*

Imagine the excitement of kicking back in front of the television set just a few short weeks from today and seeing yourself on your favorite TV program! Or, tuning in the radio and hearing yourself in a pre-recorded interview!

It may seem like a big jump from your kitchen table to the middle of that magic box, but if you have a product or service to promote, jumping on the TV/radio promotion bandwagon is easier than you ever imagined.

This course makes creating and implementing your own media campaign a reality. This book is designed for:

■ Entrepreneurs anxious to create "buzz" (and profit) with a new product or service;

■ Corporate spokespeople determined to telegraph their message;

■ Authors eager to jump-start book sales.

What to Expect From This Book

The thrill of discovering how easy it is to book yourself on TV and radio! The celebrity moments when perfect strangers look at you twice and ask if they've seen you on TV. The "Kramer moments" when clerks read your name on a check, and mention they heard you on radio in the course of promoting your product.

If it all sounds unbelievable now, just stay with the program. I encourage you to start small, booking yourself on local shows, and then when you've had seasoning and practice, going after the national shows. One thing you'll learn from this book, and your own experiences, is that publicity begets publicity.

Media Can Manifest Million$

One of the most vivid examples of media success is that of the *Chicken Soup* guys, Jack Canfield and Mark Victor Hansen whose "rejection proof" mantra and positive, energizing approach to self-promotion turned their initially obscure *Chicken Soup* book into a multi-million dollar speaking and publishing empire.

Here's How it Works:

Think of me as your personal coach, providing the *knowledge*, the *inspiration,* and detailed examples of the tools of the trade.

You will write the letters, make the calls, and show up for your radio or TV interview. It's that simple. We'll both be working together to get you all the TV and radio opportunities you can handle.

Benefits You Will Gain From This Book

- Profiting from strong sales for your book, product, or message as a result of FREE media publicity;

- Enjoying Celebrity Status when the media crowns you as an expert;

- Discovering media secrets expensive PR agents are desperate to keep hidden!

One Media Appearance Spawns Many!

TV and radio appearances have a synergy all their own. Once you appear on one TV show, suddenly the phone begins to ring and all the top shows want you as well.

Why?

Because now you are a "proven entity!"

You are now a desired guest because you are articulate, fun, and lively on the air. Producers also like a "sure thing" and feel more comfortable taking a chance on guests who've been on other shows.

Mark Victor Hansen, co-author with Jack Canfield in the *Chicken Soup* book franchise, have become millionaires and best-selling authors by mastering the art of being a great guest. Hansen shares that media people run in a small circle and word quickly gets around.

Publicity, you'll find, begets more publicity.

Media Gives You Credibility and FREE Advertising

Media interviews allow you to come across as credible and real to your target market, whereas advertising has a blatant self-promotional ring.

The Media Gives You the Credibility to Jump-Start a New Career

The TV and radio media automatically crown you as an expert and authority in your field, opening up several exciting new opportunities, additional income, and new career opportunities! Here are just a few ways the Media can set you on the road to riches:

1. As an expert visible in the public eye, corporations may seek you out for seminars and keynotes. Many speakers make over $10,000 per engagement;

2. You can launch a lucrative stream of income as a coach or consultant to individuals or businesses needing your guidance;

3. If you are an author promoting a self-published book, you can use the summary of your media exposure to:
   - Win a publishing deal;
   - Attract a top agent;
   - Make money writing articles;
   - Get better placement with distributor;s
   - Sell more books!

Mastering the art of becoming a media magician is never easier than it is today, with thousands of shows to choose from and technology just a fingertip touch away. More than ever before, TV and radio shows not only want you, they need you to fill airtime. Without experts such as yourself, they wouldn't have the ability to entertain or retain their audience base.

So realize that TV and radio shows aren't looking for ways to turn you down or keep you out. Instead, they're looking for ways to welcome you in!

More Than a How-To Book

This course doesn't just tell you what to do, but how to do it. My objective is to give you all the tools and techniques so you won't need me, or anyone else, to help you with your media campaign.

Think Like A "Headliner" Magician

If you have seen celebrity magicians in Las Vegas and elsewhere, you realize that though they both perform magic, presentation makes all the difference.

Mastering the Art of Presentation

The savvy Media Magician is constantly looking for:

- New ways to be compelling to the audience;
- Fresh approaches to a familiar situation;
- Well-rehearsed patter.
- Effective props.

Mastering the Art of M.A.G.I.C.

I've created an acronym to encapsulate many of the concepts of this book and the elements of a successful media magician.

M = Mesmerize your audience

A = Appeal to the hidden fears/desires of audience;

G = Give valuable information

I = Integrity is everything;
C= Credibility leads to happy, loyal clients for life.

Each individual letter represents such a broad concept covered at length in the course of the book.

Mesmerize Them With Your Style, Wit, & Expertise

You've no doubt know the word "mesmerize" means to "magically attract." It is taken from the name of Franz Mesmer, an Austrian doctor instrumental in the field of hypnotism.

And television is hypnotic! So is radio! Viewers and listeners are enticed to stay tuned in the form of "teasers," short segments promoting what will happen after the commercial breaks.

Your audience won't return to see or hear an advertisement, but they will return for real benefits, tips, or advice that will enrich their life.

Appeal to the Hidden Fears and Desires of Your Audience

Regardless of whether you are using this book to attract clients, sell products, or generate book sales, realize that people must be *motivated* to take any action in life.

In science, and in life, a catalyst must stimulate change. To make people want or buy what you have to sell, you must take responsibility for creating "want" and "need." Publishing guru Dan Poynter tells an interesting story in his lectures, noting that Cliff Notes are more expensive to purchase over the Internet than in a bookstore. Why? Because when students must take a test the next day, they need the information NOW – and the bookstore may be closed.

The executives behind infomercials and TV shopping networks know that their audience will happily sit in front of the television forever, putting off the buying decision, unless there is an immediate demand to buy it now. If you watch these programs, you'll note that there's a "call to action" at the end, alluding to a special discount, an extra, or another perk for making the purchase right that minute.

Behavioral psychologists note that two things primarily motivate people: that which arouses fear and that which promises pleasure. Think about what you have to sell for a moment and jot down ways your product/service might assuage the risk of pain or promise pleasure to your potential audience.

Units of Information

Most of us think people mindlessly watch television or listen to the radio, but this isn't exactly true. Viewers and listeners have freedom of choice, and can change channels in an instant. You must give them excellent content to keep them hooked.

Just as you leaned about the pain, fear, and pleasure principles above, when it comes to providing good content for your audience, experiment ways in which you can sandwich these principles together with your product and personally apply it to better the audience's collective lives.

It's best to think in units of information, and make your individual points quickly. One great way to do this is by following a "tip sheet" example when answering the host.

Tip Sheet Success!

A tip sheet is a document containing a list of five or ten "tips" that the reader can employ to gain a specific benefit. When preparing for the show, follow the tip sheet model for your verbal answers, but try to insert facts, statistics, and a personal anecdote with each tip whenever possible. Be succinct and brief when delivering these tips.

Let me give you a few examples from various industries. A tax accountant, realizing that a lot of people fear being "caught" by the IRS, might in advance prepare a bullet list of "How Avoid Raising a Red Flag to the IRS" information. The tax accountant would then answer the host's questions using these points supported by facts, statistics, etc. Conversely, at the start of swimsuit season, a fashion expert might focus on "How To Try On A Swimsuit Without Tears" tips with a host.

Interest Your Audience in Your Expertise and Product Sales Follow

Tell and sell!
- Create a perceived or real need for your product;
- Explain its benefits and features;
- Provide incentive to act now;
- Lure in potential customers with something free!

Retail managers know that "free samples" lead to strong sales. Often, it's the generous, free samples of goods that motivate people to shop or buy.

Offer a Free Tip Sheet

Short on money? Give potential customers a valuable service by sending them a free tip sheet! When you are on radio or TV, mention you will send anyone a tip sheet on your specialty that sends you a self-addressed stamped envelope. The tip sheet will have really valuable tips, all your contact information, and sent with a professional looking brochure or order form for your products. The audience will have your information at their fingertips, and you will have their address for your mailing list.

Cool idea, or what?

Be sure to follow-up with postcards or a newsletter. Studies prove the need for three contacts before establishing a relationship.

Be Credible

Do you remember writing a term paper in high school? It wasn't fun having to dig up all those musty old statistics and anecdotes to support your argument. And at that time in your life, you probably couldn't see a real-world application.

Well, here it is now, coming back at you.

Your viewers demand you deliver statistics and facts to back up your statements. Don't worry – you won't have to do more legwork than calling your local librarian in most cases. But realize that statistics make you sound credible. Make liberal use of them, especially since getting them is just a five second phone call away.

How to Get The Most Magic From This Book!

Creativity in approach spells the difference between getting on top shows or continuing to envy those who do. And though the top publicists are experts in their field and should be hired by celebrities and others who can afford them, for most of us, the basic difference between doing work ourselves and pawning it off on a publicist boils down to four crucial elements.

- Create a perceived or real need for your product. The top publicists are on a first-name basis with the producers and have an instant "in" with them. The publicists use their familiarity with the show's format when making their pitch, and good connections make it easier all the way around.

- Publicists are persistent. They make follow-up calls.

- Publicists also use the latest headlines and are careful to tie into current, newsworthy events.

- Creativity in approach is their mantra. They realize they'd starve if they took a cookie-cutter approach to their clients. Instead, they have creativity sessions with themselves or their staff to brainstorm new ways of launching clients.

Finally, in the course of our work we'll be using many of the creativity techniques I use with all my clients. In order to do so you might pick up some inexpensive creativity tools:
- Crayons or colorful markers.
- A notebook. It can be drugstore inexpensive or designer chic, but carry it with you everywhere so you can jot down ideas as they come to you.
So, what are we waiting for? *Let's get started!*

Chapter I
Getting Started!

In this chapter you will learn:

☑ Why you must position yourself as an expert;

☑ Importance of showmanship;

☑ Elements of a successful pitch letter

What is a magician? The *American Heritage Dictionary* defines it with words like "conjurer," "enchanter," and "someone who performs magic tricks to amuse an audience."

As a media magician, you will need to master all three definitions. You will be expected to enchant and entertain with your M.A.G.I.C. tricks, and in the end apply these conjuring skills to sell more products.

How Media Magicians Can Master the Art of ESP

The most successful stage magicians have an aura of mystique about them that suggest they're "other worldly" or gifted with ESP, extra-sensory perception.

Effective Media Magicians tap into the acronym of ESP.

E = Expert.

S = Showmanship.

P = Pitch Letter.

Whether you are trying to interest an editor in an article about you, publish your own article in a magazine or newspaper, or get on TV and radio, you need ESP and you need to master the art of a targeted pitch letter to a specific producer.

The magic wand of all *Media Magicians* is the pitch letter.

Importance of a Targeted Pitch Letter

The mistake most neophytes make is sending out a generic pitch letter.

Visualize yourself working as a producer for a busy media publication or show. You are at your desk, which is filled with papers and materials. You open a newly delivered package containing a pitch letter and a media kit.

You begin to read the pitch letter.

The word "skim" is more appropriate. Because you're already so busy, you are looking for a reason to throw the material in the circular file.

Does the first sentence motivate you to read more? Does it look like the sender intimately knows your show? Does the subject matter pertain to the type of segments you usually produce (i.e. cooking segments). Is your name spelled right? If not, you will toss it.

Sending out a generic pitch letter is a waste of time, energy, and trees. Target carefully!

Hollywood and the Art of the Pitch

Before I created my TV talk show I worked at various studios in Hollywood including TriStar, MGM, and Lorimar, and listened to hundreds (thousands?) of screenwriters pitch their movie ideas. A successful pitch could make a screenwriter a millionaire. If they didn't understand the elements of pitching well, they'd never sell their idea, no matter how brilliant.

Your Pitch Letter and a Hollywood Movie Poster

Executives in Hollywood spend the weekend readings screenplays and then "pitching" them to the chairman or president of production on Monday mornings. When I was at Tristar, we had one senior executive who asked a singled question in the midst of our presentations: "Tell me the Poster."

Your pitch letter must have the same elements of a movie poster: in short, it must act as a microcosm of what your segment will be about.

When you see a poster or advertisement for a film in the newspaper, you will see people laughing if it's a comedy, people embracing if it's a love story, or other elements that reflect what you will gain to see in the film.

A pitch letter must be the same way.

The pitch letter must reflect the inherent drama, comedy, passion, and immediacy of your subject.

Presentation

We're taught not to judge a book on its cover, yet most people do. That's why clothes are sold, cars sell for outrageous amounts, and people aspire to live in the best neighborhoods.

What people see is what they assume they get.

So just as you wouldn't go to a job interview in old jeans and a sweatshirt, take a closer look at your stationery.

Is it professional looking?

Crisp?

Of a good weight?

In fact, does it meet or beat the look of any stationery you've ever seen?

Stationery counts for more than it really should, but don't underestimate its ability to wow.

The Magic of Expertise

Do you only equate the word "expert" with individuals who achieve the notoriety of Alfred Einstein, Sigmund Freud, and Carl Jung? If so, pause a moment to consider the "official" definition of the word "expert" as defined by the American Heritage Dictionary:

"Having, involving, or demonstrating great skill, dexterity, or knowledge as the result of experience or training."

Now tell me! After all the time, effort, money, and energy you devoted to your field of study, can't you also be classified as an "expert in your field?"

Of course you can!

The word "expert" isn't reserved solely for dead scientists and psychoanalysts. You, personally, are an expert by virtue of the fact you have a gift to offer as a public service. And when you give good public service, individuals will buy into what you're promoting.

Position Yourself as an Expert

To get booked on a talk show, it's absolutely crucial that you position yourself as an expert in your field, literally in word and deed. Authors, as you introduce yourself to talk show producers in your pitch letter, don't introduce yourself as the "author of x." Instead, say that *as the leading expert in your field of x,* you want to help the audience resolve their issues with x."

Or, if you happen to be a self-employed attorney or an insurance/real estate/financial broker, introduce yourself as "an expert in the field of x."

Why? By positioning yourself as an expert instead of an author anxious to recruit book buyers or businessperson eager for fresh clients, you come across as an individual who wants to help the audience resolve their issues.

Talk show producers have been "burned" by guests who turned the show into a soapbox for their own self-promotion. Their objective is to find quality experts who'll both enlighten and entertain their audience. Often, these expert guests are authors or business people such as yourself. But the trick to getting on the show is in how you position yourself.

Inside The Mind of a Producer

Producers don't care if you created products or books or corporations. As they read your cover letter, producers are only interested in knowing as quickly and succinctly as possible as how you will be of service to their audience and an asset to their show.

If you can't immediately address your credentials and expertise in the first sentence of the pitch letter, it will be tossed and your efforts will have been wasted.

Your pitch letter must arrive on their desk like spring water in a draught: in other words, tailor-made to their exact needs.

Obviously, you will have watched the show to see what these needs are, and have taken the time to find the right producer to contact.

Let us imagine that you are a marriage counselor who has just written a book on the subject. You already know to position yourself as a relationship expert instead of an author or counselor.

So what should your pitch letter include?

☑ Promise of the valuable content you'll give the show;

☑ Allude to how you'll dispense expert advice and information;

☑ Include bulleted points that will transform to sound bytes;

☑ Suggestions for visual appeal (TV) and radio call-in contests;

Examples of Others Who've Positioned Themselves Effectively

As you think of ways you can position yourself to get on talk shows, consider these examples of individuals who've done it effectively.

Greg Godek is an expert in the field of romance. In fact, his moniker these days is "Mr. Romance." And his expertise in the field of dating, romance, in marriage is what keeps him a popular interview by TV and radio hosts, and fueled the sale of nearly two million copies of his book, *1001 Ways to be Romantic*.

Though Greg was probably always a romantic, pre-book his field was advertising. He became "Mr. Romance" when a class he taught at the Cambridge Center for Adult Education (outside Boston, MA) became a hit.

Sensing a big opportunity, Greg's advertising and packaging background kicked in and he positioned himself as "Mr. Romance," going on to write the book, sell it at the marketplace where authors, book sellers, and publishers meet (now called Book Expo America), and send himself on an RV tour across America.

Media Magic

Hundreds of high profile TV and radio interviews (including Oprah) resulted from the tour, and continue today. Greg was out to make his name synonymous with romance, and it worked.

Greg positioned himself as a romantic expert and success followed.

Conversely, Position Yourself as a Failure ...

Failure means major $$$ for John Fuhrman, who successfully positioned himself as an expert on the subject of failure.

Stirred to action by the rejection of his manuscript from major New York publishing houses, John turned rejection into a major achievement with the publication of the soon-to-be best-selling book REJECT ME, a work geared to the corporate market.

The book's message, based on his own experiences, maintains that if one is unwilling to fail, they are unwilling to reach their potential.

The message has definite value to the producers of TV and radio shows he appears on, as he's educating the audience on the virtues of failure: namely, that one must risk failure in order to achieve success.

John isn't afraid to admit the failures and mistakes, which actually launched his success.

Upon publication of his book and working on shoestring budget, John couldn't afford a publicist. Working on seat-of-the-pants instinct and full of ambition, John sent a faxed media release to a hugely popular radio station in San Francisco.

Good move, yes?

Well, sort of.

New to the faxing game, John hadn't realized that his colored fax would appear *black* when taken out of the radio station's fax machine. The end result looked messy, poorly produced, and a "failure" as a marketing piece.

Since the subject of his book was failure and the marketing piece came across the fax machine as poorly produced, the station thought the fax was a joke that supported John Fuhrman's claim he was a failure.

"This fax demonstrates what you are trying to prove!" he guffawed, giving John five precious minutes of high profile airtime.

John performed well and the radio station phone rang off the hook for orders!

The failure expert was a success!

Or was he?

Since the book is a best seller today, John doesn't mind revealing a bigger set of mistakes so we can learn from them.

- He didn't have a toll-free number to give to listeners when he was on the air, so they could act immediately and place the order;

- He didn't have a web site to send listeners to;

- He didn't have a distribution system in place.

Sam Horn is a best-selling author (*Tongue Fu, Conzentrate, What's Holding You Back?*) and sought-after national speaker.

Like the "Mr. Romance" expertise of Greg Godek and John Fuhrman's mastery of "Reject Me Failure," Horn has established a niche for herself in the art of using one's wits to lash back when someone says something nasty or demeaning. She's successfully positioned herself as the "Tongue Fuä" master and advises people how to respond to criticism, direct arguments, and deal with negative communications. Sam Horn's niche and enthusiasm for her topic attracted megawatts of TV, radio, and print publicity including *Readers Digest, Chicago Tribune, Washington Post, Cosmopolitan, Entertainment Weekly,* and more.

What other factors are involved in positioning yourself as an expert?

- Perseverance;
- Belief in your concept;
- Creating a unique platform.

Experts Dress For Success

In the 1960's, a popular television commercial featured a handsome man in a white coat. He held a bottle of aspirin and stated with deep-voiced authority that four out of five doctors recommended that brand to their patients.

If the viewing audience stopped to think of it, they'd probably realize that the man was an actor, not a doctor. If they thought about it some more, they'd probably want to know the name of the study, how objective it was, and possibly, about the one doctor in five who disagreed the brand was the best.

But because the actor spoke with such authority, and cited a statistic that on first hearing sounded impressive, viewers never really questioned the advertisement.

Experts exude confidence and speak with conviction! They convey these elements as soon as they walk into the studio or first speak with the host for a remote radio interview.

Projecting the voice of authority is crucial in getting an audience to buy what you have to sell. Rehearsing your main points well in advance of the show will help you master this voice. Later in this chapter, I'll reveal some magical techniques to make this happen!

Experts Are of Service to the Audience

Experts answer the audience's questions and promote their products and books in a subtle yet succinct and calculated fashion. They've rehearsed the message they want to present in a way that will help the audience and motivate the audience into buying what they're promoting. In the course of answering questions with expert advise, they are careful to:

- Mention their product or book by name;
- Give the audience a chance to see what it looks like;
- State where it can be bought.

Experts Act Humble

Sometimes a host will preface the interview by saying something like "John, tell us about your new book."

John might be tempted, of course, to tell the audience all about it. That's why he went to all the time and trouble of preparing the materials and pitch letter to get booked on the show in the first place, right?

He should resist taking the bait!

Jumping into one's promotional self is tempting, but instead, take the expert stance and turn your attention to larger, more universal issue of what you are promoting.

Media Magic

Authors are notoriously guilty of speaking about their book instead of the larger issue.

On my TV show I featured a fiction writer who turned the segment into a non-stop commercial for his book. Since the author's book was about a kidnapped child, he would have been better off focusing on the larger issue of kidnapped children, engaging the audience's emotions by citing statistics of how many children are kidnapped each year, the emotional plight of a real-life family who endured the abduction of their child, etc.

To elicit interest in his book among the audience, the author could have made frequent references to his title, such as "I based my book, *The Kidnapping,* on the real life story of this family" or "I used the same psychological profile of this kidnapper in my book, *The Kidnapping.*"

Experts Make Liberal use of Facts and Statistics to Engage an Audience

Attorney Alan Dershowitz is a master at finding a universal core as a platform for his many books. When he was on my TV show promoting *The Last American Jew,* he attracted a wide audience despite the limitations inferred by the title.

How did he do it?

- He created a need for Americans to take a closer look at the issue of inter-faith marriage by quoting statistics and trends;
- He provided valuable tips for families dealing with the issue of inter-faith marriage, drawing from his own personal experience with his son and daughter-in-law.

Inter-faith marriage is a difficult issue for many, but viewers watching the show and concerned about the growing statistics could take comfort in the fact that many families have successfully worked these issues out, and be motivated to buy the book for more insights and helpful advice.

Now that we've covered the "E" of ESP that *media magicians* use in a pitch letter, we'll discuss the "S" - showmanship.

Let The Show Begin!

In your busy daily life, wouldn't you look fondly upon an employee who anticipated your exact needs and put together a project without your having to lift a finger?

Talk show producers are no different.

When you proceed to write your targeted pitch letter, realize that television is very competitive, and producers are very busy.

You can increase your chances of getting booked if you think through your proposed segment before writing the pitch letter.

What does this mean?

Obviously, the first step is to watch the show and get a strong sense of the kinds of guests they usually book, including the kind of **visuals** or "shtick" (e.g. gimmick) guests employ to drive home their point. Try to do as much thinking and planning as possible before sending the letter. Your goal is to get a "yes, please be our guest" from the talk show producer. If they see you've done your homework in terms of seeing the show as an appropriate target and writing a compelling pitch letter, you've practically got the gig.

Now, there's one more thing to do.

Put together the show segment.

Me? Put together a show?!

In the media classes I teach, many students are surprised that a "guest" would do the runaround work of putting together a show segment for a producer, without any guarantee that they'll even get on the air.

In fact, producers see guests as products. When selecting an expert for a show, the producer's behavior is very much like yours when choosing between two similar items in price and quality, but one comes pre-assembled.

Which would you prefer?

Watch Shows For Inspiration!

The *Mars/Venus* TV daytime talk show is always great for getting exciting show ideas. Watching it, one senses that the producers are eager to keep the show quite visual and dynamic. One recent segment featured an exercise guru with a jump rope, demonstrating the "rump jump" in which he lifts his rear end from the floor each time the rope goes around.

Another expert, this one promoting a book on palm reading, proceeded to mark up the hosts' hands with a magic marker, tracing their love lines in bold, black ink.

Elements of Packaging Yourself for TV

Once you've watched and targeted the show you want to appear on, you will want to position yourself for the appropriate segment.

Chefs, for example, might find a good mix on many of the morning shows, both national and local.

Psychologists, either those with a book to promote or simply to increase their platform, might want to target talk shows such as *Jenny Jones, Sally Jesse,* or

Oprah. In this venue, there is an opportunity to showcase one's expertise.

Returning to the example of chefs, finding the name of the specific "cooking segment" producer is important. You need to call the show in advance to identify the appropriate producer and send this individual a targeted pitch letter.

Realize, also, that there are many different ways that chefs - or anyone with something physical they can demonstrate – can promote himself or herself on a show. Ease and time saving tips, or a new twist on an old theme, makes you stand out.

Jamie Oliver, aka "The Naked Chef" and author of the cookbook of the same name, appeared on many talk shows to promote his book and engaged in activities with each host. With Rosie O'Donnell, he was cute, clever, and beat out a drum-like sound with the utensils at hand. On *Good Morning America*, again he was also cute and clever, but on this show he involved all the hosts in a dessert recipe. Of course, Mr. Oliver had a "brand name" publishing company behind him (Hyperion) with press people who set up the interviews. He never did the same thing twice, which is key. If you are a chef, suggest either creating a dish on air, or bringing in something delicious and describe how it's made.

A seasonal approach is always a good idea for chefs, and anyone else who can use the turning of the earth as a marketing angle. Valentine's Day, for example, presents the opportunity for:

- Chefs to show off decadent desserts and candy;
- Department store representatives to show off romantic gifts;
- Authors to promote books on romance;

Media Magic

The main point is to think of a way to make your promotion look visual and unique, not to mention fun.

Entrepreneurs who help people organize, for example, might want to bring in a trash bag of "stuff" they pulled from someone's desk, or talk about the average weight of a woman's hand bag, etc.

Put Experts Together!

The format of the Oprah show changes often, but many times the show focuses on one controversial issue featuring guests/experts from different perspectives.

If you are a psychologist who wants to get on the show and deal with an issue that crops up in your practice (e.g. anorexia) you might want to consider taking the extra step of finding a (formerly) anorexic guest who overcame the disease with your help, an author on the subject, the mother or relative of a victim of anorexia, and a dieting model.

Send the producer a winning pitch letter with the information on the guests you've assembled and why the topic is timely and beneficial to the audience. If you do this legwork and you as well as your guests pass the credential test, chances are you will make the cut.

Be Controversial

Dan Poynter, a well-respected author, consultant, and speaker in the publishing industry takes the concept of putting together a show even further. He suggests his clients put a show together, but also add the ingredient of controversy.

"If you are pitching a diet book," he says, you will want to put a show together with three people who've read the book, two of whom became thinner and healthier as a result, and one who thinks your diet is a crock."

While some experts may cringe at the thought of having to deal with a negative person amidst all the other pressures of being on television, Poynter does (can't resist the pun) have a point. Controversy keeps an audience's attention. Riveting an audience's attention and keeping them at the edge of their seat, is the very thing a producer wants to do.

Beyond that, the negative guest gives you, as expert, the perfect opportunity to win them over by quoting an impressive number of facts and statistics. In this way, you will be addressing the concerns of any skeptics in the audience, and will be winning them over in the process.

Controversy can also intensify after the show has aired, increasing the potential to be invited back.

Magic of the Perfect Fit

Do you remember the story of Cinderella? Unless the foot slid perfectly into the glass slipper, the handsome prince would not accept her.

As a child, the magic of this parable might have eluded you. But the surefire way to book yourself on TV and radio talk shows lies in positioning yourself as the perfect "Cinderella" fit.

1.   Watch TV and listen to Radio!
     ■ Your objective is to find guests similar to yourself!
       This is not the time to break new ground and
       convince a show they need someone of your type!
       Stick to what they regularly feature, and what
       their audience expects to see! But use your

freshness and unique presentation or format to
attract their attention.

2. Take notes on guests similar to yourself and in these
notes write:
- What was good about them? What did you learn?
    What you could do better? By this I mean if you
    were them, what would you do or say to add
    more value to the viewer's experience?
    How do you do this?

    Don't waste your time or anyone else's by
    spending irreplaceable time to get on shows you
    are not right for! Don't be a round peg in a square
    hole.

3. Don't be a time sucker!
- Your objective here is to view shows and target
    the best so you can personalize your letter to the
    producer and refer to specific shows.

- Identify the producer responsible for the guest
    (call the station).

    Larry James, former Associate Producer for
nationally syndicated *Men are from Mars, Women are from
Venus* radio show, defines the "perfect fit" as a guest with
the authority to speak on relationship issues in an
engaging way. Though the show was primarily about
romance and love between couples, an enterprising
would-be guest who positions himself or herself as having
knowledge of any of the many areas of relationships
would be asked to appear on the show.

Marisa D'Vari

Summary

Getting on TV and radio is easier than you think, but you must be proactive. Having a new product or book isn't enough. Neither is simply being charming. The magic of *Getting Booked Now* is that you've created the perfect alchemy between your talents and a show's needs. So, have you decided to go the Media Magician's way?

This week's assignment!

☑   Refer to yourself as an expert in casual conversation. Just get used to the feel of the word on your tongue.

☑   Watch talk show television and listen to talk radio with an active eye and ear. Note the questions hosts asks and how guests respond.

☑   Create a sub-folder called "shtick" in the notebook you should always carry with you. Document the way that guests visually telegraph their message and brainstorm ideas on how you can do the same for what you're promoting.

Start Considering Yourself an Expert Now!

In the seminars I teach, I've found this exercise to be of value in helping authors and entrepreneurs orient themselves as experts.

Media Magic

Try This Exercise:

■   Create an opening sentence in a mock pitch letter in which you introduce yourself as an expert, followed by three ways in which you can help viewers.

Go ahead, just write the following: My name is _____ and as an expert in _____, I can help your viewers

1.

2.

3.

Show Ideas For TV

■   Spend some quality time thinking about how you can make the concept of what you are promoting more visual for TV. Think of panel discussions with like-minded or controversial experts, props, film clips, etc

1.

2.

3.

Show Ideas For Radio

■   Now think of ways you can make a radio show more attractive as a guest. Giveaways, contests, and quizzes are always good!

1.

2.

3.

Chapter 2
Media Release Magic

In this chapter you will learn:
- ☑ Importance of a tabloid headline
- ☑ Creating a release that doubles as an article
- ☑ Where to send your release

In the film *King Solomon's Mines*, Stewart Granger knew lunch was ready when African drums began to rumble. Of course, it took him a few moments to realize that *he* was to be the main dish!

Throughout history, every culture has developed their own means of communication. Africans had the drums. Ancient foot messengers risked death if they dared deliver bad news. Children (at least, until the arrival of wireless communication) would have fun thinking they could really communicate with empty orange juice tins and a length of string.

Today, we have the media release.

Media Release 101

To launch yourself on talk shows you must target your market and cater specifically to their needs.

You must offer information they can actually put to good use!

You must make the information easy to digest and absorb.

You must motivate them to buy.

No one needs extra clutter in their house or office, but if this "extra clutter" will make their life easier or fulfill a demand of the job, they'll be interested.

Media Magic

So right now, think of the end-receiver of your press release as a busy individual who won't even give your *headline a second glance* unless it promises immediate satisfaction and off the bat, appears to be something they can use.

That having been said, I'd like to point out what goes into a media release and what you need to do to make it alluring to your end-receiver.

The Scheherazade Concept

"Scheherazade" is the name of the fictional princess in a book called One Thousand and One Nights. She was a beautiful woman who married a king with the unfortunate habit of marrying a new wife each day, consummating the marriage, and then beheading her.

In order to survive, Scheherazade decided to tell the king a story with a cliffhanger ending each night, so that she'd be allowed to live until she could "finish" the plot.

In the end, Scheherazade was successful, and you will be too, if you incorporate her technique into your writing.

The trick – and this really is a trick similar to Scheherazade – is to tease with tidbits of information you know that your end-recipient can use, let leave the recipient yearning to know more.

In one of the many informative articles on his web site (http://www.mrfire.com) Joe Vitale speaks of his efforts to promote his self-published book *Hypnotic Writing* (now incorporated into his book, *CyberWriting: How to Promote Your Product or Service Online (without being flamed)*)

Vitale bought a mailing list of all the writing magazines in the country and sent a one-page news release to each. Several printed a half page article about his book, taken word for word from the press release. Had he paid for this kind of advertising, it would have cost hundreds or thousands of dollars. But his cost was simply standard postage.

What did Joe Vitale do right? He created a media release that didn't immediately get trashed, for one thing. Second, he provided the kind of copy that could easily and effortlessly be transcribed by a busy editor with little money to pay writers into "content."

The Media Release Breakdown

1. A media release, as with all the forms you will be creating in our time together, is an item to be skimmed;
2. Liberal use of key bullet points makes it easy to skim;
3. Winning headlines are short, startling, and read like those found on newspaper tabloid covers;
4. If necessary, add a subhead to partially explain, but primarily incite more curiosity;
5. The first sentence following the head or sub head should be sharp and selling and paint a visual "word picture" that tells the reader what you are promoting in an instant! Be sure to seamlessly weave key information here, such as the five "w's" of journalism (who, what, when, why, and how).

I'm a personal fan of using a lot of white space on the page and bullet points to attract the eye. Fashion savvy readers will remember being told that certain designs flatter different figures. Just as you take care to dress in a flattering manner, dress your words with an attractive frame!

I'm also a fan of the one-page press release, which has become the industry standard. Believe me, if you've got your prospect reading the first page, you've convinced them. They don't need to spend valuable time reading more!

But what if you need more space for explanation, as in the case of a technical issue? Go ahead and send a two-page release, but edit ruthlessly. A good way to do this is to use imagery and visualization to convince yourself that every word is costing you ten bucks, editing out all but the most succinct, sexy, selling copy.

Formatting Basics

Media releases follow a specific form. Some freedom is allowed, but for the most part you will want to create a template with these fixed areas:

■ "For Immediate Release" in uppercase letters in the upper left corner.

■ "CONTACT" with the name and telephone number of a person to call for more information (along with fax, email, web, etc).

■ For Authors Only: Give book information in a box at the bottom left of the release, including:

☑ Book Title
☑ Publisher
☑ Publication Date
☑ Format (i.e. hard/softcover)
☑ Price and page number
☑ Book's ISBN

While faxing doesn't cost very much, you are wasting trees unless you know enough about the recipient to think they can use you and your material on their show.

TV talk show hosts, like myself, receive a flood of media releases every day. Most of us would admit we barely read past the subject line. When we do, it's because the subject is *appropriate to the show* or can use the information in some way. There are a lot of "mass fax-ers" who make it more difficult for individuals who've carefully targeted a show to get noticed.

On the next page, you will find a media release I created for Shameless Promotion Month, a holiday I created with Chase's Book of Days.

Insert your contact names, address, and information and follow the key points in the example as a guide to developing your own release.

Media Magic

1000 Main Street · Anytown, State Zip
(area code) phone · fax
mdvari@deg.com · http://www.deg.com
CONTACT: (Your name & phone number here)

For Immediate Release
Today's Date

"Tune in with your Inner Egomaniac"
September is Shameless Promotion Month!
5 Tips to Prosper in a Downsizing Economy

Current Date– Your City, State
"The only way to succeed in a slowing economy is to self-promote," says
Marisa D'Vari, author of the new marketing book Media Magic: Profit and Promote with
FREE Media Promotion.

D'Vari is also the creator of Shameless Promotion Month, a national holiday
dedicated to entrepreneurs, authors, business owners who must rely on self-promotional
savvy to survive. D'Vari has created a tip sheet to help shy self-promoters kick-start the
celebrations, and encourages everyone to celebrate their success stories in her free ezine
by sending an email to Shameless@deg.com.

Five Tips For Instant Self-Promotional Gratification

1. Create a "signature" for your email. Never send an email without a standard template
advertising the benefits of your business, book, or service.

2. Never leave home without a business card! To make sure they're always with you,
put them in your purse, pocket, all coats, briefcase, pda case, & gym bag.

3. Talk shows want you! Book yourself on TV and Radio! You don't need a publicist,
and it's easier than you think! (See http://GetBookedNow to learn how).

4. The names in your database are dollars in disguise. Create an ezine with content and
keep in touch!

5. Write for profit! Approach the editor of your community newspaper or trade
organization's newsletter, and write free articles tacitly promoting your expertise!

###

Note to Publishers and Authors: put your own book info here
Author's Name, Publisher, ISBN #
Pub Date, # of Pages, Cloth or Paper cover

Make The Media Release Newsworthy!

Brainstorm way to make the media sit up, take notice, and say, "*wow!*" Or, at the very least, give them an incentive to feel as if their audience needs to hear what you want to promote.

Keeping Current

Another way that you can make your media release newsworthy is to tie it in with current events in the news. If the presidential elections are coming up and you've written a book on the topic, draft a media release that looks at the situation from another angle. If you are a fashion designer, you might consider writing a humorous or factual "tip sheet" aimed at nominees and their spouses, suggesting what fashion is "in" and "out." This is how many of today's fashion commentators (seen on the TV morning shows and on cable shows) got their start.

The basic concept is this: The word "news" doesn't have to mean front-page news at all. It just has to mean some new study or piece of information that will make the media take notice.

Send Media Releases Often!

Media releases are great when you have real news! Joe Vitale, entrepreneur, author, and creator of the website http://www.mrfire.com, updates the "profit center" article section of his web site weekly and sends the media regular, relevant updates using http://www.imediafax.com.

John Kremer, book publicity guru and author of 1001 Ways to Market Your Books, advocates the 9/18

Media Magic

Rule. Which is to contact the media nine times in
eighteen months. The point is that you bolster your
credibility when you are not a one-shot wonder. So
when you brainstorm, also consider how you can
lengthen the duration of interest for your book as a
product.

A restaurant owner, for example, can send a
release about a new menu or lower prices.

When To Send Releases

Does the day of the week you send the release
really matter? The answer is really less important that
creating a dynamic headline, but wisdom suggests that
Tuesday – Thursday are the best days for softer news,
Friday is great for weekend highlights, and Saturday is the
easiest to get placement.

Where to Get Producer Contact Information

The reference section of your local library is your
best source for up-to-date, free information on the how/
what/where to contact TV and radio talk show
producers, print editors, newspapers, and periodicals.

You can purchase your own set of the various
media directories but each one is well over a hundred
dollars and they are quickly outdated.

List of Popular Media Directories

National PR Pitch Book
Bulldog Reporter
Bacons'
Burrelle's
Gale's
Gebbie Press

Media Directories for Sale

Again, you can buy the directories listed above, but they really are too big, outdated, and heavy for use. But if you were to buy a directory, make it Publicity Blitz. It's published twice a year on CD-Rom by Bradley Communications. Their phone number is 800 989 1400 x 713.

Media Research Tips at the Library

1. For efficiency, you will want to have watched enough TV and listened to radio to know the shows you want to target *before* you get to the library.

   Call first, and ask to speak to the reference librarian. Make sure they have most of these directories available for your use, and ask when they've been updated.

2. Once you get to the library, remain focused and keep your target audience clearly in mind! With thousands of shows to choose from in these directories, it's quite easy to go off on a tangent! It's best to start with the category you believe best suits your target market.

3. Bring a laptop computer with a good database system such as Act or Goldmine to record the information, or plenty of coins for the Xerox machine.

Media Magic

Summary

Writing an effective media release is a creative endeavor, one that should be approached in that spirit. Remember that your objective is to get the release read. Though it's true that media outlets want good information for their audience, you will have to take the effort to "serve it to them" in an appetizing style.

This includes the way the words are arranged on the page, the amount of white space on the page, and the information itself.

Your Assignment:

☑ Think of five different "hooks" you can use for what you're trying to promote in a media release. For example, you might find a holiday that is a good fit, a current event, etc.

☑ Spend quality time crafting a "grabber" headline.

☑ Write a Media Release "body" that has the three necessary elements for success:

1. A "teaser" style that compels the reader to continue reading instead of tossing the release;

2. Your contact information and printed permission to use the material without further contact from you;

3. Information that can be immediately used in a feature or article.

Chapter 3:
Sidewalk Hustle: How to Get Booked on TV and Radio

In this chapter you will learn:

☑ The art of observation

☑ Honing your pitch letter

☑ Brainstorming a gimmick to use on the air

In Manhattan, few individuals can beat the innate savvy of a sidewalk street hustler. Sidewalk hustlers have the ability to size people up in an instant, and always seem to know the score. As soon to be self-promoters, so do you!

Sidewalk Hustlers Are Observant!

Hustlers survive by their honed observation skills to make their extremely lucrative living. They can size up your personality and ways to make you buy when you are just turning the corner.

How?

People reveal themselves through dress, behavior, body language, eye contact, and an overall "aura" that surrounds them. Once a hustler sizes up a viable mark as a likely conquest, he has them made. Hustlers know just the right words to separate you from your money.

How will mastering this hustler's skill help you land a talk show?

The answer is disturbingly simple. A hustler knows exactly who they are, what they want, and after sizing you up in a half-second, how successful they'll be in getting something from you.

Guests who've successfully booked themselves on talk shows know who they are, realize that guests are to serve and not be served, and after watching a show, will be able to sense if the show will see them as a good fit and if so, what segment to appear on and what angle to take in the pitch letter.

Step One
☑ Watch/listen to all the TV and radio shows you want to be on, and if you see other guests that are similar to you in what they have to offer as expert, put them on your "yes!" list.

Step Two
☑ When you find a show for which you'd be a good fit, make note of the type of segment, the host interviewing the guest, and try to find the producer's name at the end of the credits. If you can't spot it, call the show and ask.

Step Three
☑ Watch and listen carefully to shows on your "yes" list. Closely note these elements:
> ☑ What is the standard interview time?
> ☑ How many questions does the host ask in that time period
> ☑ Do most TV show segments feature the guest doing something demonstrative?
> ☑ How are the guests positioned?

Positioning of Guests

An expert invited to appear on Sally Jesse Raphael as a guest (and weighted voice of authority on whatever issue is being discussed) is expected to act more aggressive than an expert on Oprah's show. Because the slant of the shows is so different, each pitch letter would require a specific slant.

The Pitch Letter

The purpose of the pitch letter is to introduce you and showcase your expertise to the shows! Begin by performing the steps listed above, which include watching the various shows, taking note of the various segments, and deciding how you can best fit in with the show's style.

Fresh and original is always good, except when it comes to getting booked on talk shows. They want you to be just like everyone else in your field of expertise who's been on, but with a slightly fresher, more original spin. Don't try to break the mold or else producers won't know what to do with you.

Bewitch Them!

A pitch letter must make a convincing argument that you will be an entertaining guest, as well as an "expert" whose advice and message will appeal to the demographics of the show.

The pitch letter is a carefully crafted document specifically designed to grab the interest of a busy, often distracted producer. To Increase the odds of its effectiveness your own pitch letter must: and discreetly trumpet the following:

☑ Why *you* are the best authority to speak on your subject;

☑ Why the subject would be of interest to the show's audience;

☑ Why the audience needs the information you are giving NOW.

Everyone wants to get on Oprah's show. People often use the title of this show in a generic fashion. When most people say "Oprah" what they really mean is that they want to sell more books.

To sell books, you'll have to research the show that attracts your target audience. Rebecca Morgan, author of the best selling business book *Calming Upset Customers*, reports that since Oprah's audience didn't fit the profile of buying her books, her appearance on that coveted show did little for her.

The Tone of Your Letter is Important!

It's important to match the tone of your pitch letter to the radio or TV show. I can't emphasize this enough. If it's to *Oprah*, address the tone of the show (educated, somewhat sophisticated, female-oriented, literary). If it's to Jenny Jones, your tone should reflect high drama, conflict, emotion, and a bit of shock-value.

Grab A Producer's Attention With Startling Opening Sentence

The first paragraph of your pitch letter should be designed to elicit the interest of the producer. Example:

Subject: Cat-owners Have Nine Lives!

Did you realize that cat owners live x% longer than humans without pets? Or that petting a cat will slow, calm, and regulates a human's heart rate?

Hello, my name is XYZ and I'm the author of XYZ and an expert on cats and the benefits they bring to the lives of their owners. I'm enclosing a copy of my book and media kit, and would very much like to make a guest appearance on your show.

Available to join me is the victim of a heart attack and his physician, who will testify how having his patient buy a cat aided his recovery. I will call you next week to discuss the show in more detail.

Here's another example, a bit more sensational in nature.

Subject: *You May Be at Risk for a Mysterious, Debilitating Disease!*

In the headline, you've alerted people that they may be at risk for this "mysterious" and "debilitating" disease. Hypochondriacs are hooked ... now it's time to get the attention of Mr. And Ms. Average.

You want to construct your next sentence to make people think that by having these innocuous symptoms, they may actually be experiencing the beginning of that debilitating and mysterious disease you alluded to.

Your lead paragraph might read like this:

"Doctors agree that X disease starts insidiously. You are feeling fine, then bang! You can't sleep ... your neck aches ... and not even your trusted family doctor can explain why feel so darn tired all the time.

You may be at risk for disease X!

Untreated, disease X can worm its way into your life, sucking out every ounce of joy and vitality until you feel like a dried-up, listless shell of your former energetic self.

In the show, I'll discuss how your audience can avoid this dreaded disease, and if they do happen to feel they have it, how it can easily be reversed without the expense of doctors or hospital bills.

Emotional and Compelling

You've presented an emotionally compelling message to the audience (and producers), grabbed them in the gut, and now its to explain why you, and you alone, are the best-qualified *expert* to discuss disease x.

The last paragraph should list your credentials. For the disease example above, any kind of medical degree, articles, lectures, studies, etc. is helpful. If you don't have this kind of credential, explain your expertise by association (e.g. how you cured a loved-one or friend of this disease).

If you live in a media city like New York, L.A., or Chicago, and the show you are pitching to is based there, you may want to state that you live in that city and are available on short notice. This is how Dr. Ruth Westheimer got her start, by filling in for guests who cancelled last minute on talk shows. Be sure you leave a cell or beeper number where you can be reached immediately!

You need to highlight contact information. Even if you have your email, web, phone, fax, and address on your stationery, you will profit by including both your email and your phone number in the body of letter.

Why?

It's about saving time and thinking about everything so the producer just picks up the phone to schedule you as a guest. And when you are scheduled, do not neglect to ask for an emergency phone number to the station.

Summary

Since you can't be in the producer's office in person, sending a tailored pitch letter to a specific producer of a specific show is the next best thing.

You must religiously watch the show and take notes.

Be sure to note guests who speak on a similar subject and comment on them in your pitch letter, not necessarily what they did wrong, but the extra things that you will do to inform or entertain the audience.

Be sure to follow-up, which is one of the most crucial elements of getting booked. If you get voice mail, try again. If you have done your research and believe you're perfect for the show, and are the sort of guest the show usually features, be persistent! It will pay off.

Your Assignment:

☑ Watch a talk show you think you'll be appropriate for and as you watch, create a form for yourself.

Have columns that include details such as the number of segments per show, if a certain host conducts an interview for a certain segments, if most of the guests have "shtick" (a gimmick) to keep the show lively.

One example of shtick can be an author who wrote a book on Tarot, giving tarot card readings to the host or members of the audience. Also be sure to write down the names of producers you see as the credits scroll. If you can't make out their names, call the show.

☑ Create many of these forms, study them, and decide your three best shots. Write a specific pitch letter to each, matching the tone of the show in the "voice" of your letter, and be persistent in calling back.

Chapter 4
Elements of Your Media Kit

In this chapter you will learn:

- ☑ Purpose of a media kit
- ☑ How to fill a media kit
- ☑ What to do if you need to bolster your media kit

A media kit is to entrepreneurs and authors what a wax doll is to voodoo witch doctors. In short, it's a roughly hewn approximation of your essence.

Even though producers can't see you in person, they still base their judgments on first impressions. Most publicists and guests trying to book themselves on talk show send a pitch letter clipped onto a media kit, which I'll explain in a moment.

The presentation value of your letter and your media kit are each important. Before beginning your media campaign, try to factor in stationery and printing, as these items quickly add up. Remember, since you can't be there in person, your stationery and media kit are representing you, and you'll want them to look the part.

In addition to ordering personalized letterhead, you'll want to create a professional looking media kit. A media kit is simply a folder that attractively displays material that will reinforce the fact that you are an expert guest.

Producers do judge a media kit by its quality. Basic print shops such as Kinkos, Sir Speedy, and Copy Cop will have many samples to show you. Compare shop and find the best kit that suits your taste and budget.

The quality of the information inside the media kit is equally important. Note that the exterior media kit, as well as the quality reproductions of the material inside the kit, are quite expensive. But don't feel as if you're "wasting" a kit by sending it to a producer. If you've taken the precaution of identifying guests the show has had on in the past who are similar to yourself, and see that you're a perfect fit, you have a good chance of getting on the show.

Listed Elements of the Media Kit

- ☑ B/W picture (name and contact info on back);
- ☑ Media release(s);
- ☑ Articles by you or about you;
- ☑ Sheet of potential interview questions;
- ☑ Your bio;
- ☑ Reviews of products and/or books;
- ☑ Book jacket cover, picture of product;
- ☑ Testimonials;
- ☑ Brochure
- ☑ List of media appearances;
- ☑ Video or audio tapes of you;

1. Picture

Pictures should be black and white, and the appropriate size should be 5x7. The producers like to get an idea of what you look like, and therefore, the photos should be current, within the last two years. Shop around for the most inexpensive way to reproduce them. In general, buying in volume is the best way to go. In addition, include your name and contact information in the back of the picture in case it's separated from the media kit. Create clear labels with your name and phone number on them, and simply stick it to the back.

2. Media Release(s)

It's a good idea to include any media releases you've written about your product, service, or book so that the producer can get a fuller sense of your expertise.

3. Reprints of Articles (written about you)

Has someone written an article about you? *No?* Then start soliciting one! I'm sure that you live in a community with a local neighborhood paper. This is an excellent place to start! Just call the editor, say that you live in the neighborhood and want to help the community by giving them information on "Topic x," with "x" representing what you want to promote.

4. Reprints of Articles (written by you)

Regardless of whether you are promoting a book or a product, there are many opportunities for you to write an article. Check with your local librarian about where you can access trade magazines in the appropriate field. Though these magazines may not pay much if at all, the "clip" (the word journalists use for a reprint of the article) underscores your credentials through third party endorsement.

5. List of Questions

In the idea world, what questions would a TV or radio host ask you that would show you and what you have to promote in the best light? Start by putting yourself in the TV or Radio host's chair. Think about the information you would want the host to ask about.

Write up a list of Q & A. This format helps you expand on material used in the release. The other benefit to having this on hand is that if you are a guest, and the host doesn't have the time to completely review your materials, you can hand them a conversation starter.

6. Bio
Make it fun and upbeat (and quick!) to read. Tempt the producer with juicy bits!

> Paragraph 1: sell yourself and your experience
> Paragraph 2: quantify previous experience
> Paragraph 3: list professional affiliations
> Paragraph 4: list educational accomplishments

7. Book/Product cover or packaging
Authors take note! Getting hundreds of copies of your book jacket cover will never be cheaper than when your book is going through its first printing. Alert your publisher to the fact that you need at least five hundred extra copies. In all likelihood, it should not be more than $100 for this amount, possibly less.

What will you use the covers for? Everything! You can fold them and use them as a self-contained media kit, and you can make them into postcards. You can also use them as a cover for your audiotapes.

But instead of sending a book with a face value of $18.95, you might simply fold the cover up and put it in your press pack, including a fax-back form to send the book out immediately upon request.

8. Testimonials
Savvy media mavens start collecting endorsements (these are also called "blurbs" for book jacket covers and testimonials for businesses and services) as early as

possible. They can be used in advertising and marketing. You'll find that some people, even celebrities, are very agreeable to looking at material, and others very reluctant to attach their name to anything. But you'll never get an endorsement unless you ask, so do so!

The best time to ask for a testimonial or endorsement is when you receive a compliment. Let's say that you gave a talk or performed a great service and someone worth quoting pays you a compliment. Ask them, right there, if they'd mind putting it in writing.

If you can be helpful in some way to the individual you're asking for an endorsement, that's always the best option. What goes around really does come around, and if you can't be helpful to the person who gives you an endorsement, make a note to return the karmic favor to someone else at the appropriate time.

9. Brochure

Many businesses have spent time, resources, and money creating a brochure. If you are promoting a service or product, here's the place to include it. Brochures generally have the longest shelf life of anything else you produce. Because of that and the expense I would recommend consulting with a professional.

10. Media List (if applicable)

If you have made appearances in the past this is the place to list it. Important details include the name of your program, broadcast date, program type, and if a recording of the show is available on demand.

Begin your list when you get your first show date!

Alternatives to the Conventional Media Kit

Media kits can be expensive to produce, costly to mail, and very time-consuming to stuff. If you are on a budget, never send a kit out without contacting the producer first to make sure s/he is expecting one. Sent unasked, most kits wind up unopened in the circular file.

Even if you're trying to promote a business or service, consider writing a book, self-publishing it, and sending it out instead of a media kit. Why?

Consider these numbers.

It costs about $18.00 to send my media kit out, and this figure does not include postage or a book. It does include the cost of the color printing of my articles and other related items.

If you publish your book in a large quantity, say 5,000 copies, each book can cost under two dollars each.

Of course, you'll still need to send some marketing material with the book. But most people consider books something of value and they tend to keep it around, whereas kits are often tossed. Sometimes, if you call back to see if it was received, you'll be horrified to learn it was tossed and that they'd like you to send it again.

Also consider sending media kits via Fedex or Airborn express, even if it's two-day delivery. The cost isn't that much more than normal mailing, and it helps make your media kit stand out.

According to publishing guru Dan Poynter who spoke at the Publisher's Marketing Association's publishing university in Spring of 2000, online media kits are the trend of the future. In his talk, he explained that when reporters call, they don't have to wait for you to overnight a photograph of yourself. They can download it directly from your site, and access articles, taped audio interviews, and more.

Everyone with a web site should have an online media kit. You can see mine at http://www.dcg.com and when you scroll to the bottom of the left column, you will see a link for my online media kit.

On it, you will find the following information:
1. Notice of speaking engagements
2. Back cover information for my products;
3. Testimonials from readers;
4. My bio
5. Press requests for books;
6. Cover art and author photo to download

You might also consider using the latest technology to create a welcome message via an audio link.

Though online Media Kits are great time and money savers for authors and others anxious to get booked on talk shows, you must have a physical media kit as well.

Why? Many reporters prefer not to go online, or their modem is too slow. Others just like to have something physical in their hand.

The future of online press kits may not be here yet, but it will be soon and when it does, be ready for it!

Summary

A media kit showcases your expertise to give the audience your expert advice on a topic. Make sure that you include only material that is applicable to what you plan to promote. Articles, either written by you or about you, should pertain only to the issue at hand, or exclude them.

Once you begin to create your media kit, arrange to always have a few on hand that you can send on a moment's notice.

It's also a good idea to send a media kit to yourself, so you can see how it will be received by the producer. Are the stamps neat? Does the label look professional?

One trick I employ is to write something intriguing on the outside of the envelope to whet the producer's curiosity. Sometimes I use stickers or a rubber stamp. Anything to make the package scream "open me!"

Your Assignment:

■ Consider what articles may be appropriate to add to your media kit. If you don't have any, start now! Contact appropriate trade organizations or a local paper and "pitch" them a story. Explain that you'll be happy to do the article gratis in exchange for a "tag" box indicating your name, your email, phone, etc.

■ Start to price various printers and talk to a few graphic artists. Shop around for the best price. Also consider contacting a college near you and seeing if a graphics student would be interested in designing your logo or stationery.

Chapter 5
Spellbinding the Media Into Finding You

In this chapter you will learn:
- ☑   How to have the media call you
- ☑   Resources on where to list your information
- ☑   How to create an effective advertisement

While there's always a thrill involved with doing the work, sending the material, and getting yourself booked on TV or radio, sometimes it's just great to have the media call *you* and ask when it's convenient for you to be on their show.

In the best of all worlds, this occurs when you've achieved a certain degree of fame and notoriety in your field. Perhaps a flurry of articles has been written about you or your company, or the field you're in is red hot.

Such was the case of publisher Angela Adair-Hoy, who is constantly delighted by the attention her popular ebook and publish-on-demand oriented web site (http://www.BookLocker.com), and ezine get by the media. Adair-Hoy credits the media with much of the success of her endeavors, expressing the often-verbalized truism, "publicity begets publicity."

In the Hollywood film industry, Ken Atchity, an author and successful literary manager, runs a relatively small operation yet is consistently quoted on the front pages of the industry's two big daily trade papers, Hollywood Reporter and Daily Variety.

Neither paid for placement, but by virtue of their proactive, pioneering stance in their respective fields are often front-page news.

So how can you make yourself sought-after by the media?

1. Be innovative in what you do;
2. Position yourself as a credible source of information to the media;
3. Be accessible;
4. Develop a relationship with the media.

Developing a relationship with the media is easy when you develop a template for your actions. The first step is becoming familiar with the reporters in national and local publications or TV and radio that cover your beat.

Send them a letter or email, but always from the vantage point of suggesting that you will be an expert source for them when they're on deadline. In other words, stress the "Magic You."

When you make contact, tell them that you respect their keen reporting and would be happy to help them out if they need someone of your expertise to round out a story.

You can suggest you have access to:

☑ Industry trends as a basis of being in the business for so long, or representing such prestigious clients, etc.

☑ Story ideas for them, based on actual questions from clients, readers, or others that suggest a universal need for that information;

☑️   Other sources, since journalists like to use quotes from several sources, especially if they represent polar sides of an issue;

☑️   Recourses where they can find data and statistics quickly.

Then, of course, you can always follow the advice of my friend Mark Levy, author of *Accidental Genius: Revolutionize Your Thinking Through Private Writing*, and "try easy."

What's easy in this scenario? Save money and time by letting producers call you!

Though TV and radio producers sometimes play hard to get, they are always searching for guests and rely on a variety of resources to get them.

One of the most widely used resources is Radio-TV Interview Reports (RTIR), a monthly publication sent to over 5,000 media bookers free by Bradley Communications (800.989.1400 ext. 713). The pages are filled with house-created advertisements of people such as yourself who are determined to get their message out on the airwaves, so to speak.

People I have interviewed see RTIR as a tremendous value for the following reasons:

☑️ You are assigned to a RTIR staff producer familiar with the needs of TV/radio producer(s) to create the copy and "look" of the ad, giving you a professional appearance;

☑ Your RTIR rep knows the persuasive copy necessary to "sell you" to the media;

☑ Your time commitment is minimal. All the media producer has to do is pick up the phone and call you to schedule an interview;

☑ You double your time and effort allowing producers to book you directly from a credible resource while you pursue them individually.

Another benefit: Perceived third party endorsement by creating a single, expertly produced advertisement that has a wide distribution to people with authority and power to put you on the air.

RTIR is not "free publicity" though it attracts free publicity. How expensive? Constant promotions and special deals at trade shows seem to keep the prices fluid, but a good rule of thumb is that appearing in six issues is around or over $1500. Before sticker shock sets in, consider you will save money by:

☑ Reducing costs mailing your pitch letters;

☑ Saving on the cost of stationery reproduction;

☑ Using your time more wisely for profitable activities rather than the typing and envelope-stuffing that are part of a media campaign;

I've identified some other values in advertising in RTIR as well:

Emotional Value

A lot of people are emotionally resistant to self-promoting. They find it difficult to make follow up calls, which is the only way you will ultimately book yourself on the air. It's too easy to self-talk your way into thinking:

- No one wants you on the show so why are you wasting your time;

- What if they're rude and hang up on me?

- Why call? All I ever get is voice mail

And I'm sure you can add dozens of more reasons to the list. Having producers call you is one way to overcome self-doubt.

Get a Sample Issue!

If advertising and copywriting isn't your field, I recommend that you give RTIR a try. Money saving packages are cheaper and better, say those I've interviewed, than a one-time placement. But if you still can't afford RTIR, here is some ad-building advice.

Types of RTIR Advertisements

The rates are broken down into one-page and half-page ads. To my mind (and budget), the half page ads are much less expensive and seemingly just as effective as a full page.

Publishers and prolific authors have the benefit of buying a full page, and featuring as many of four of their titles. If you are a publisher with a tight niche, such as Michael Wiese, the publisher of my previous *book Script Magic*, you can feature four books since they books will all be about film, screenwriting, or directing.

If your books are not related, an advertisement featuring four books can look crowded and misdirected.

The key is to attract the eye and make for easy reading.

Five Key Elements of a Successful Ad

RTIR has mastered the art of the eye-stopping advertisement. When you look at the pages, you will note that the ads are characterized by:

- Tabloid style, attention-yanking headline;
- Bullet points & white space;
- Benefits to the audience;
- Credentials;
- Picture of promoter doing something interesting!

Yearbook of Authors and Experts

Mitchell P. Davis and Broadcast Interview Source, Inc. offers a publication called the Yearbook of Authors and Experts, which comes out once a year and similar to RTIR, is given free to the media.

Kelly Bliss is one Yearbook advertiser who's had great success. A psychotherapist, author, and columnist, Bliss designs her own ads and advises potential advertisers to use a lot of bullet points and avoid paragraphs.

Unlike RTIR, Yearbook advertisers are advised to turn in camera-ready advertisements.

I'd advise going through the book, seeing what ads "work" for you (in terms of which ones your eyes are drawn to) and creating a composite ad based on the elements of the ads you liked best.

Like everything else you've learned in this book, a successful result hinges upon how well you target your market, how well you understand the appeal of what you have to offer, and creative brainstorming, all of which requires a certain degree of homework.

Summary:

If you have a day job and can't be promoting yourself twenty-four hours a day, seven days a week, taking out an advertisement in an appropriate magazine may be the way to go.

Be aware that an advertisement is worthless unless you make it absolutely irresistible for the media. This means, focusing on the benefits the station and its audience can get from featuring you as an expert guest.

Smart, savvy media magicians will ask for a free copy of the publications so that they can study the ads and position themselves accordingly.

Your Assignment:

■ Get copies of the publications listed in this chapter and flip through them, pretending that you are a talk show host. As you flip, use a paperclip or sticky flag to identify the advertisements that catch your eye.

As you notice the ads that catch your eye:

Media Magic

1. Prioritize the most important aspects of ads you liked, such as:
- layout of the page;
- the picture
- the headline
- the copy
- the subject matter

2. Design your own advertisement by putting together elements in; the advertisement that caught your eye. Whether you decide to use it or not is immaterial. What matters is having a concrete advertisement before you that will allow you to focus as you plan the rest of your marketing materials.

Chapter 6
Immortality Spell: Create a Holiday

In this chapter you will learn:

☑   How holiday creation gives you celebrity stature

☑   How holidays motivate producers to call you

☑   How to create a holiday (*psst! It's free!*)

Do you remember the first time you heard of "Grandparents' Day?"

When the cards hit the drug store stands, the reaction was mixed. Some thought it was a conspiracy on the part of Hallmark to increase profits by creating yet another holiday on which to send specialty cards. Others assumed the holiday had always, but never before received its share of card buyers and media attention.

When I received the honor of judging the Focus National Screenwriting competition sponsored by the Kodak film company & Nissan motors years ago, I remember my bewilderment when the mayor of Los Angeles proclaimed the day of the awards "National Focus Day."

How could anyone, I asked myself, create a holiday? Even the mayor! When he left office, I wondered, would the Focus holiday stay on the calendar?

Now that I have a half dozen holidays credited to my name, many celebrated internationally and printed on calendars in dozens of languages, I can assure you that you don't have to be a mayor of a major city to create a holiday.

You can create your own holiday!

How to Create a Holiday

One of the two sources are Chase's Book of Days, which you can find in the reference section of your local library, or order/view online at http://www.chase.com, or John Kremer's "Celebrate Today," a book that can also be found in bookstores, the library, or online at http://www.celebratetoday.com.

Why Create a Holiday?

Creating a holiday gives you a "news worthy" item to promote! Media people are jaded. Sending a release simply announcing your web site is born, or that your book has gone into another printing, will land in the circular file.

Media magicians know that to excite TV and radio producers, they have to:
1. Think visually;
2. Think of a gimmick that would excite the TV/ radio audience;
3. Think of a way the TV/radio station can use your material to seem as if they're doing a service to their audience;

If the above list seems as if you are doing the work for the station producers, guess what? You are exactly right! I can't emphasize enough, the more work you do for a producer/booker in terms of strengthening their bond with their audience, the more eager they'll be to have you on the show.

So How Does Creating a Holiday Tie In With All This?

First, creating a holiday gives you a tangible, newsworthy reason to send a media release. On a slow news day, if your holiday looks interesting they'll call you and the resulting chat can lead to more publicity and product sales.

Even if you don't send a release, many producers just thumb through *Chase's Book of Days* or John Kremer's *Celebrate Today* as a matter of course. They'll call you and arrange an interview.

Be Prepared

Once you do create a holiday, you should create a "holiday folder" near your phone, filled with talking points you can use in your interview. You will also want to mark your holiday on your calendar so you can arrange to be home.

Once, when I found myself out of town, I left the number where I can be reached on my voice message, and received over a dozen calls I took on a hotel treadmill.

If you can afford it in terms of time and money, you should also create a web site that will act as a reference for people who want more information on your holiday, and/or create a free "tip sheet" that people can request with a self-addressed, stamped envelope.

The tip sheet should have your contact information all over it, and if you sell products, should include an order form as well.

Media Magic

If you do sell products, you'd be wise to invest in a toll free number, so that you can give out the toll free number during the interview so people can call and order your products over the phone.

Ethel Cook, a Bedford, Massachusetts based productivity coach, found that establishing her "Do It Day" for Chase really thrust her into the media limelight, especially where radio interviews are concerned.

The holiday takes place the first Wednesday after Labor Day every year since 1993 and without lifting a finger to do anything to get media attention, she gets a dozen calls from radio stations this day, hoping to interview her.

Cook also prepares a media release with her contact information on it so that she can fax or email it to stations after they call. The fax gives stations her background, but more importantly features suggested questions. The station will then have Cook's information to give listeners when they call in.

Summary:

Creating a holiday is a great way to have producers call you without the expense of advertising or the trouble of trying to contact producers individually.

To be effective, you must have your materials in place. This means considering building a web site, buying a toll free number, creating products, and creating a free tip sheet that you can send out to people who send you an SASE.

When you register your holiday, create a folder of key materials at the same time. These should include:

- ☑ Media Release;
- ☑ Question and Answer Sheet;

Marisa D'Vari

- ☑ Tip Sheet;
- ☑ Free Booklet (with product order form);
- ☑ All of the above posted on your web site.

Your Assignment:

1. Go to the library and read Chase's Book of Days, John Kremer's Celebrate Today, or both.

2. Note on your computer or on a notepad holidays that you can "piggyback on." Remember, these holidays are like Christmas. No one owns them.

While you can't say anything like "I've created xyz day," you can say, "in honor of national xyz day I am presenting ..."

Ask yourself: *what ties best in with what you have to promote?*

3. Before you leave the library, use the copy machine to copy the form at the back of the holiday books so you have the tools to create and submit your own holiday! Be sure to note the (very early) deadline for the following year's calendar.

Chapter 7
Talking Points

In this chapter you will learn:
- ☑ How to sell & promote effectively on the air
- ☑ How to generate talking points
- ☑ Idea Reeling for a hook

How would you like to wake up one day and in the course of that single day, catapult yourself to a best-selling author status?

This happened to Gregory Godek, author of the perennial *1001 Ways to Be Romantic.* After teaching years of adult seminars geared to helping men and women bring more romance into their lives, Greg decided to package his message in a book. To find a publisher, he registered to attend Book Expo America, a marketplace for publishers and bookstores.

Godek's dark good looks reinforced his romantic message, and as an added hook or signature feature, he began to wear a rosebud in his lapel for public appearances. But as he was walking in to the convention center, he realized he didn't have a rose. A hotel worker rushed to bring him one, but instead of the bud he expected, Godek received a long stemmed red rose.

At the convention, people quickly caught sight of him, the rose, and his book. "Hey, can I have one!" almost everyone said as he passed through the crowds. The media, always on the lookout for a good news story, interviewed him, he attracted the attention of a publisher, and a deal was made.

The "magic" could have stopped there, as it does for so many thousands of books that live briefly and die quietly.

What made Godek and his book a success?

Answer? The strength of his "hook" and the magic of his "message," in combination with his ability to package both. In short, Godek knew how to "tell and sell" on the airwaves that resulted in notoriety and massive sales.

As a TV host, I can testify that the biggest mistake most guests make is that they fail to shape and hone their content into an enticing hook. If a guest only talks about themselves this is a boring interview, and the audience is not engaged. Be sure to convey message points backed up by facts, statistics, and personal anecdotes. Guests must create an insatiable need for the audience to go out and buy into whatever they're promoting.

Unfortunately, most guests don't fully prepare for a TV or radio interview. Regardless of whether they're self-confident or nervous, many guests feel as if they don't need to do more than have a glass of water at the ready should they develop a dry mouth. This is short sighted and a precursor to assured failure.

There is a crucial difference between **promoting a book** and **talking about a book.** The magic lies in three little words:

- ☑ Hook
- ☑ Message
- ☑ Motivation

The key to a successful and profitable on-air interview is preparing "commercials" for your message that don't sound like commercials at all. You want to create exciting, succinctly-wrapped "information packets" in which you give viewers and listeners information they want and need. You want to introduce your product or book as the most direct way viewers/listeners can attain this helpful information.

Hooks? Messages? Motivation?

You are probably thinking you were just supposed to chat with the host about your product or book!!!

Start rolling up your sleeves, because this chapter is all about the tools of the selling trade, specifically how to arouse the interest of the talk show producer as well as the potential audience.

Selling Your Message

A persuasive speaker can always sell their message. Whether they're pitching a book or their consulting services, the seed is planted in their delivery, and continues through to the back of the room where a table is handily arranged with products or brochures.

In this situation, the audience has a chance to feel the product offered or read all about it, and the time to learn about it in depth.

But from their cars or living rooms, the audience can't skim a few pages of your book or try out your product or service to see its fine craftsmanship and quality. You have to compel the audience to want to buy your book.

To sell them, you will have to knock them out with a one-two punch. First hook them in the gut, and then prove all the reasons why they desperately need what you are trying to sell. Be quick and succinct, giving this information in a thirty-second time frame.

Marisa D'Vari

The Hook

Audiences are thirsty for entertainment and knowledge, in addition to quick, easy methods of self-improvement.   And you only have a moment to catch their attention.

Simply stated, a hook is a snappy, visual, emotionally compelling one-liner that will grab an audience's interest immediately.

Here's one example of a great hook: the description of a movie in *TV Guide?* It's a one-liner description conveying a sense of what the story is about. It does this by:

1. Describing the genre (i.e. love story, adventure, etc.);
2. Describing the roles of at least two key players and/or their predicament;
3. Is emotionally compelling.

Finding then Refining Your Core Message

It may seem like guests chat with TV and radio hosts without any real purpose, but much preparation is needed for even a few seconds of fame.

Don't expect to go on radio or TV without an agenda. Spokespeople know that the surefire key to confidence, a great performance, and lots of $ales can be boiled down to one word: *Your message.*

It's not enough to simply talk about why you wrote the book or why you started your business or service. No one cares about *you.* They care about what your book, product, or message can do for *them.* This is why it's crucial to always position your message from the potential consumer's point of view.

For a successful TV or radio interview you will need to find, hone, and perfect three key points and support them by evidence in the form of facts, statistics, anecdotes and personal stories.

Easy Ways To Create Key Talking Points

Every interview can include millions of listeners/viewers, and for your own marketing purposes it's best to prepare key talking points as if you'll be addressing skeptics who need to be convinced that your product, book, or service has value and will solve their problems.

How do you accomplish this? By backing up each point with facts, statistics, and more.

Begin this way: once you complete this exercise, you will have all the material you need for an effective message!

1. Write down your three message points horizontally on a piece of paper.
2. Beneath each, write the following words vertically beneath each of them.

Evidence
Analogy
Facts
Statistics
Quotes
Anecdotes
Personal Experience

If this sounds like homework to you, relax! If you're hooked up to the Internet, you can get this information in a matter of minutes. Or you can call the reference desk of your local library and they'll be happy to help!

Marisa D'Vari

If you have seen one of the TV shows I hosted, or anything on C-Span, you might have been surprised to see so many authors fail to motivate their audiences to buy their book. You can bet I tried as hard as I could to make their material sound enticing, but the guest was simply a talking head.

Sadly, it's also true of many of the chefs I interview for my TV show, *A Taste of Luxury*. While a great majority of chefs are fun, energetic, and dynamic, it usually takes media training to coax the creativity that made the chef a "celebrity" onto the camera.

Hopefully, you are beginning to absorb the concepts in this book and are developing a sense of creating a compelling need.

Core Message Points

When Helen Fielding of *Bridget Jones' Diary* fame, was on my show, she created a compelling need by comparing the very English Bridget Jones to the American character of the then-hit TV series *Ally McBeal*. By making this association she was telegraphing the message that the book *must* be bought by single women with boyfriend problems. Not only will single women relate to the main character, Fielding implied, but they might learn some valuable tricks as well.

Fielding's core message point was that through the character of Bridget Jones, women should accept themselves as they are and laugh at their imperfections.

Messages and the Subconscious Mind

Your hooks and messages will be used in every piece of your marketing and presentation material. This may include:

- Media releases;
- Pitch letters;
- Talking points;
- Tone and focus of your media kit.

At this point, it may be helpful to outline some of the basics to the creative process.

Four Stages of Creativity

People often think ideas 'come out of the blue.' Possibly, but brain researchers have another theory. The model presented below originated with the German physiologist and physicist Hermann von Helmholtz and was expanded upon by the American psychologist Graham Wallas in his 1926 book, *The Art of Thought*.

Stage One: Preparation

Think about what event triggered *you* to write the book or create the product or message. Talk to people about why they bought it, or what interests them in it. Examine what you have to sell from all perspectives. Be diligent in looking at competitors and note why what you are promoting is superior.

Stage Two: Incubation

This is the "Behind the Scenes" phase, when your subconscious mind takes in all the preparation you did above and works on it silently, like the clock on your computer, while you turn your attention to other things.

Stage Three: Illumination

This is the Aha! Eureka! I've got it feeling we all crave.   Seemingly out of nowhere, the myriad of different pieces fall into place out of nowhere and you are ready to precede full speed ahead with focus, direction, and purpose.

Stage Four: Implementation

At this point, you are ready to sit down and put pen to paper, build prototype, or start brainstorming your messages in earnest.   Remember to keep it:
- Universal
- Emotionally gripping
- Timely

Selling products on the air is as much about the journey as it is about positively affecting the financial bottom line.

Magic of The Magnet Message

Magnets are tools of attraction, and sources of wonder and fascination since the beginning of time. Savvy magicians have long taken advantage of how magnets spellbind a crowd.   Media magicians would do well to use the power of the magnet to make sure their message has that lasting spellbinding effect.

The objective of this chapter is to help you ensure the audience remembers your product or book long after your segment is finished.

It's brainstorming time.   Let's roll up our sleeves and immerse ourselves in a creativity session.

What's *your* message? How are you going to make it *stick* in the minds of the audience?

Universal Images and the Collective Subconscious

When we create our Magnet Message, our objective is to tap into a universal "switchboard." The concept of a universal switchboard was created by psychologist Carl Jung to describe a collective source of memories we all unconsciously tap into. It's a phenomenon that allows some writers to write believably from the perspective of someone from of another culture or sex without any research at all. It's how readers and film audiences have immediate connection to situations they have never experienced before.

The entertainment industry looks for films with the potential to tap into this universal switchboard. *Rocky*, the Sylvester Stallone film, is a case in point. Love, hate, sex, passion, jealousy, survival, safety, these are all issues that arouse our universal interest.

Keep asking yourself what you are promoting and how to grab an audience's interest in a very deep-rooted, emotional way?

I was giving this talk in a seminar, and during a brain storming session, an insurance salesman said that he focuses on the universal fear of a man leaving his family destitute by not planning for their future financial care.

Another attendee wrote cookbooks, and didn't think that her book offered an appropriately "serious" magnet message.

We brainstormed a bit, and it turned out her cookbook was vegetarian in nature. The magnet message we hammered out was how to live longer by eating healthier food. I encouraged her to dig up facts and statistics that support how a vegetarian lifestyle can help individuals.

Magnet Messages & Movie Posters

Remember my reference to a movie poster? A movie poster is designed in words and pictures to convey a powerful, emotion-packed universal message. Copywriters want anyone who sees the picture and short text to sense the entire story in a glance.

How is this possible? The artists are tapping into universal images everyone can intuitively understand.

Like a movie poster, your Magnet Message must tell a story!

Look in the newspaper or a billboard to examine the poster or advertisement. What does the poster tell you? One of the posters for *Gone With The Wind* featured Clark Gable carrying Vivian Leigh while the plantation Tara burned behind them. The image suggested passion and danger against the backdrop of war.

Let's go from films to the corporate world. Consider the imagery in these popular corporate logos. Prudential Insurance uses a logo with a rock, suggesting stability. Coca-cola's energetic, red and white logo offers a slogan assuring consumers "it's the real thing." The concepts resonate long after the image is gone.

What visual mental image does your Magnet Message convey?

Find Benefits, Then Create Magnet Messages

The real "magic" of conveying an emotional message on paper is to master the subtle but crucial art of viewing your book or product specifically in terms of its *benefits to others.*

Media Magic

Producers and audiences alike want to know how your book or product can make their life more fun and enjoyable or help them out of a difficult situation.

To fulfill their needs, you will need to convey a Magnet Message that conveys every benefit of what you are promoting in a glance or an instant.

Now you know what the Magnet Message is and what it needs to convey. But how do you get one?

Magic of the "Idea Reel"

One of the most effective brain storming tools around is the "Idea Reel," which I adopted from the traditional Mind Mapping example developed by Tony Buzan and other brain researchers in the 1970's.

The exercise is limited to five minutes, which forces the subconscious mind to create a game plan very, very fast. As the subconscious mind responds to color, invest in some crayons and get ready to make some magic!

Scientific Basis of Idea Reeling

Tony Buzan discovered that the brain is made up of two distinct halves. The left brain is the "editor. " It's the voice insisting on order, and that tells us that all must be in order, that paragraphs should have a beginning, middle, and end, etc.

The right brain is the happy, creative child, telling fantastic stories in no apparent order.

The Idea Reel works because by drawing a picture, we accomplish several things:

- We shut out the "editor" left brain, allowing only pure creative thought;

- We avoid inhibitions or the tension association of "work" and "school"
- We open ourselves to the fun, energy, and color in relation to the project at hand;

The Idea Reel separates the critical left part of the brain from the creative right, allowing creativity to flourish in a free and open environment.

When you were a child, you were naturally creative, with brilliant, creative ideas. You thought nothing of coloring outside of the limits. Then, you went to school and the colorful stories you told as a toddler didn't go over well with your first grade teacher.

"Stories need a beginning, middle, and end," teacher would tell you, a lesson drilled into you over and over again. You found yourself knee deep in a world of documented reports, lined paper, and structure.

Now that you are an adult, much of your innate creativity has been suppressed with feelings of responsibility. When your right brain dares to unleash a wildly creative thought your logical left brain (the"editor") is quick to censor it.

When you use the Idea Reel, you are unleashing your creativity. Drawing out your idea not struggling to structure it into proper English. Since the creative right brain rules art, music, and everything fun and creative, it feels comfortable giving you great ideas without fear of censorship.

When you've harvested all the fruit the right brain has to offer, then it's safe to allow your left brain in to edit and evaluate what's appropriate for your audience and the marketplace. The left brain weeds out the brilliant from the merely good.

Idea Reeling In Action!

Since you are already reading this book and are familiar with many of its concepts, let's use the material in this course as an example.

At this point, my objective in preparing the Idea Reel is to generate newsworthy angles regarding this material that would interest a talk show producer and motivate the producer to invite me on his or her show.

As every talk show has a different audience, I can't use the same "pitch" for every show. But I can create a pitch that would work for women-centered shows like *The View*, Controversy shows like Sally Jesse Raphael, and late morning shows like Regis.

But since the material is geared toward business, my most targeted audience would be watching well before the typical workday starts at nine am.

This is where I'll make the most sales, so I'd Idea Reel this first.

To begin Idea Reeling, draw a circle in any color crayon in the middle of a sheet of paper. Inside the circle, draw a symbol or the words representing your central issue.

In this case, it is getting entrepreneurs and others in need of low-cost publicity strategies to tap into the resources of this book.

Don't worry about supporting your ideas with facts, statistics, personal anecdotes, or anything else at this point. Just work as quickly as possible and use many colors as your draw tangents from the circle, each offshoot containing a scrawled written word representing an idea or a symbol of that idea.

Marisa D'Vari

Some Mental Steps

We are all individuals and our minds wheel in different directions. But my mind works in a way that searches for the universal factor first. So, crayon in hand, I ask myself what is the largest issue looming in the news?

Today, it happens to be the economy and the massive job cuts every corporation seems to be making.

It also means that self-employed professionals are facing an ever-dwindling list of prospects, and more than every before, must tap into the power of free publicity to overshoot their competitor.

Talk show hosts are well aware of the above, and will naturally agree with my angle.

After I Idea Reel ideas, I'll find the best of that particular spoke (i.e., the self-employed early morning crowd) and perform Internet or library research in order to back up the findings with statistics, facts, and quotes.

I'll weave the above into a perfectly executed letter geared toward the 7-9 am local and national talk show hosts, both radio and TV, and then move on to my next targeted segment (i.e. viewers of controversial and women's' shows).
lipstick, ties, or cigars.

Try It Yourself

Okay! Get your supplies of crayons and paper before you, and find an area where you won't be disturbed. I'm going to explain the procedure first, and then give you some examples and exercises so you will know how to Idea Reel when I'm not with you.

Now:

1. Get out your colored pens and uncap them!

2. Visualize the imagery of what your message is all about.

3. Cut out any "mind-yapping" that detracts from your focus.

Idea Reeling is all about personal freedom, but there are a few key rules you might want to note.

1. Be Ready To Work Fast!

Working quickly is the key to creating an effective Magnet Message, since Idea Reeling promotes intense "creativity bursts" by forcing your ideas on paper in a short period of intensely focused time.

To make sure you physically set a time limit, I suggest you purchase a kitchen timer or stop watch. Five minutes is the longest any one Idea Reeling session should last.

2. Start with Your Concept's Central Image

Let's use the example of this book to create a catchy Magnet message. We'd start by drawing a circle in the middle of the page, and inside, seeing and feeling the essence of what people hope to get from this book.

I created this book to help business individuals and authors tap into the power of free publicity for the price of the book, instead of the tens of thousands of dollars they'd have to pay top publicists. This course incorporates the disciplines of several other fields in order to bring buyers solid information on how to design their own media campaign, including advertising, marketing, copywriting, promotion, and even how to perform effectively on TV and radio.

Marisa D'Vari

I want readers to feel excited and energized reading this book, produce real results with their media campaign, yet not overwhelm with information.

So, with this in mind, I'll create tangential offshoots listing all the benefits followed by features of this resource.

If you're working along with me, on your own worksheet or notebook, the image displayed should be a circle, which will eventually be filled with quickly drawn, colorful lines which radiate out in spoke fashion.

Working fast, jot down any benefits that come to mind as swiftly as you can! Scribble, use symbols, just get it down in physical form and don't let your crayon pause for a moment!

Once you've exhausted your ideas or your timer has gone off, stop and transcribe your squiggles into sentences that you can read. Mine look something like this:

Consumer Benefits of Investing in Media Magic: Profit and Promote with FREE Media Placement

1. Convenient, "all in one book" information;
2. Do it yourself PR without expensive publicist;
3. Friendly, you-can-do-it narrative voice;
4. A-Z campaign details from Media Release to Media Interview;
5. Interactive book with examples and exercises;
6. Reasonably priced for value;
7. Reader should feel energized and empowered;

You can spin a web of slogans and phrases from each one of the benefits listed above, but your Magnet Message has to be all-encompassing enough to support each phrase listed. Otherwise, you are just leaving money on the table by failing to make potential customers aware of all you offer.

For example, creating a Magnet Message based on the fact that this book is merely affordable would negate the very real fact it is easy and fun to read, offers high content, offers exercises and tips, etc. Likewise for creating a Magnet Message out of the "friendly voice." What good would a friendly voice do if your investment yields no value?

Idea Reel Exercise

Now, your turn.

Your objective is to list the benefits of your book, product, or message to consumers.

Begin by drawing the circle as previously shown. As you do so, feel the magic as limit ideas immediately pulsate from your brain, down your arm, and directly onto the page.

- Fill the center circle with the message you are trying to communicate.
- Pause a minute to see it, feel it, and sense it.
- Make it as emotionally vivid.

Remember that whatever Magnet Message you come up with, your audience will have to share that exact visual, emotional image.

Your words must create an image!

Our brain "thinks" in pictures. Just reading the word "lemon" makes us pucker!

Avoid Mind Yapping

Fight the temptation to censor yourself or even "think" when you idea reel. You want to write down *every* thought or image that comes into your mind, uncensored.

After The Idea Reel

Before you end your session, take the precaution of transcribing your Idea Reel into text, either hand written or a computer file. List your Magnet Messages in terms of their benefits to the audience, and store your Idea Reel someplace safe so that you can refer to it again. Are there any common themes emerging? Can you isolate one or two that stand out more strongly than the rest.

Realize that Idea Reels are not carved in stone. Create as many as you like. But you might find it helpful to save them for future reference and analysis.

The subconscious mind works in curious ways, and later that afternoon or evening when you are reviewing your Idea Reel, you might find that the idea you were ready to dismiss provides the twist you've been looking for all along!

And once you have that twist, turn it into a catchy slogan!

The Catchy Slogan

The pop music group, The Beatles, became millionaires by mastering the art of the catchy slogan in their music. You can do the same thing for your business or product by creating a slogan in words.

San Francisco based Literary Agent Jillian Manus often mentions the importance of slogans in her speeches. In one session, she told her audience that she longed to have a catchy slogan attached to her name, but couldn't find anything to rhyme with "Manus." Then one day she decided to use her first name, Jillian.

The result?

"Make a million with Jillian." The most perfect Magnet Message an agent can have.

Dan Poynter, a publishing consult, uses his own name to promote his newsletter, *Publishing Poynters.*

Marcia Yudkin, marketing guru, is well known for her short, succinct ezine, The Marketing Minute.

Creative ideas are everywhere. Try tying yourself, product, or service in with popular movies, lyrics to popular or classic songs, or even TV chefs. After all, didn't the title of that great American classic, *The Galloping Gourmet,* clearly give a sense of show's style?

Make (gasp!) Assumptions About Your Target Buyer

We're told never to judge a book by its cover, *yada, yada, yada.* But to save time and money, you have to literally define your target buyer. There's no sense in creating a marketing message to the beat of a hot teenybopper song if your target customer is mature men.

So go ahead, judge that book by its cover! Assume the most stereotypical mindset you can about the people representing your target.

In college, I had a chance meeting with an executive from one of the top chains catering to middle-class, middle-America guests.

"See that man wearing the polyester pants with the imitation leather belt?" he said. "That's my customer!"

There was no need for this executive to a create glitzy, high tech campaign to attract business tycoons because that was *not* his customer. The hotel executive knew that price, the appearance of a clean room, smiling front desk clerks, and overall helpful service combined with a bargain price would keep his rooms full and his guests return customers. And that's exactly the approach the hotel chain took in their marketing campaign.

If you own a store that sells fur coats, you can make several assumptions about your target customer. She probably reads upscale fashion and lifestyle magazines such as *Town and Country*, travels to ritzy resorts, and fashion-savvy. More important from a psychological standpoint, you might dare to assume they have a "keep-up-with-the-Jones'" mentality, which you can use to your advantage by selling "snob appeal."

Beyond Than Assumptions, Walk a Day In Their Shoes

That's right! If your target audience has a different income level and interest than yourself, why not "walk a day in their shoes?" Imagine that you earn their exact income and have the same type of buying behavior as your target audience. Think how'd you spend the day, spend your resources, and actually try it out! Go to the stores or bookstores they'd frequent and eavesdrop on what they have to say about books or products similar to yours.

When you write your Magnet Message, the first hand experience you would have gained will make your message that more poignant!

I can't stress this enough, but always keep your target market firmly in mind as you brainstorm a "Magnet Message." Make your message as specific as you can. That store selling fur coats, for example, might use the snob appeal slogan "we provide luxury merchandise for a discriminating clientele."

If you operate a family-style pancake house, you'd really want to telegraph the feeling that your pancake house is a fun place where kids are welcome. In our collective imagination, looking at a pancake house from a kid's point of view, it's a place to get wild with syrups and eat sweet-tasting food that's fun to eat. In many families, it's also the only "dining" experience outside of fast food, and has its own rituals (sometimes free crayons and toys to keep kids occupied during a wait, etc).

What emotion or sensation do you want people to experience when they think of you and/or what you're promoting? Capture the essence in a slogan!

Summary:

Develop a way to hook the audience before you are interviewed for radio or TV. In a TV sit-com, this is the opening situation that draws you into the show. In an infomercial, it's when the announcer reminds the audience of all the pain they might experience because they're out of shape, and then "hooks" them by explaining how easy and fun it is to lose weight and look fit by purchasing an exercise machine.

You also must develop and rehearse magnet messages and talking points in advance of the show. Develop your lead message with facts, statistics, and personal anecdotes. The best-remembered messages are those that strike an emotional chord in listeners.

On both radio and television, your objective should be to promote yourself and sell your products or services, but do it in a way that makes you a valuable guest to the audience. You want the host to ask you back. Realize that hosts talk to each other, and if you "ruin" the show for a host by turning it into a commercial for yourself, word will get around!

Idea reeling is an excellent way to create the kind of slogans and messages that will help you target and appeal to your core market.

Your Assignment

■ Write a paragraph in which you describe your core market in detail. Remember that no one product appeals to every single person.

■ Idea reel the best approach to reach that market. For example, the words you use and the hype level would be different when marketing to teenagers than adults.

■ Idea reel the elements your core audience will value most in your product or service, and rank these benefits.

■ Support each of these benefits with facts, statistics, and a personal anecdote to illustrate the point.

Chapter 8
Selling Sizzle

In this chapter you will learn:
- ☑ How to psychologically sell to your audience
- ☑ How to telegraph benefits
- ☑ Why details make *all the difference*

One can learn a lot about Magnet Messages from studying a TV Infomercial. Once you get past the announcer's hyped-up voice, you will see how even the most simple infomercial stresses the *benefits* a viewer will enjoy by purchasing the machine.

One of the best selling Infomercial products is an abdominal machine; so let's use this as our example. Here are some notes that should be of value to you.

Infomercial List of Ab Machine Benefits
1. Just *minutes* spent with the machine a day will turn you from fat to slim;
2. The workout is *effortless* and can be done while watching a favorite TV show;
3. Storage is no problem, as the device can fold up and fit under the bed;
4. It's a good investment as it can be used and personally adjusted by each member of the family;
5. The price is divided by three easy payments.

Note that the typical infomercial usually features an attractive and fit man or woman, effortlessly working out with the machine, which is designed to appeal to a person on a visceral, emotional level. Only a true skeptic can resist the product's appealing benefits, which include looking great, eating one's fill, easy product storage, and low monthly payments.

Psychology of Selling

QVC and other selling channels stay in business because their hosts get results with high volume sales. Why do they get these sales?

They have a profile of their customer base, know their tastes, and track sales to see what sales techniques work best.

QVC is also well aware of the power the hosts have to generate excitement and create a buying frenzy. To QVC's loyal audience, the hosts are like a glamorous but very approachable TV star they welcome into their homes each day. The hosts don't just "hawk" the QVC trinkets, they hand sell them as if they were showing off exquisite diamonds on black velvet in Tiffany or Cartier.

Each item sold is described in detail, and it's details that drive sales. Beyond the details of the appearance, a ruler is usually held up to the item so that the TV audience can get a very real sense of its size. Note, too, that the hosts are well-skilled in painting emotionally charged word pictures, usually centered around how great a member of the TV audience will look wearing the item, how adaptable the item is for casual and dressy wear, a "first time ever" deal, and the ultimate closer, they only have a few items left in stock and aren't sure if they'll be getting more in.

Details Drive Sales

The hosts aren't just selling earrings to the audience, they're painting a very visceral word picture of what it would feel like to wear those earrings at a variety of functions, and what it would be like to walk into a party and be the envy of all the women in the room!

The host's identification and appreciation for the product is key to strong sales. Because the most female viewing audience relates to the female hosts so strongly, her approval and delight in the product means a lot to them.

Often I've tuned into the various shopping channels to observe the art of the sales pitch in one of its most compelling forms. For the most part, items are shiny, glittery, fun, feel-good-now items that are strong impulse buys.

Details Turn Ugly Sweaters into Fashion Items

Every so often, I've seen some real horrors being hand sold as if they were priceless jewels. One I vividly remember was an ugly, cheap-looking beige sweater that looked as if it had been pulled from a thrift store bin. In fascination I watched as the sales woman very convincingly outlined dozens of the sweater's "valuable details" that suddenly made me take notice.

As I listened to her voice radiating appreciation for the "gorgeous sweater," the sweater began to transform into a thing of beauty. If there's a lesson to be learned in this it is realize that your tone of voice, the way you touch your product or book, and other non-verbal messages often speak more convincingly than words.

Phrases That Work!

At all times, make sure that you are appealing to the emotions of your audience. Consider some of the emotional states below, and try to brainstorm words that will appeal to them.

One of the secrets of effective advertising is to use the kind of emotion-packed words and vivid imagery that will slyly hypnotize your audience into buying into what you have to sell. Use descriptive words that will make them see, feel, taste, touch, and almost smell the benefits you're selling.

For example, sales people know that if they want to sell someone an expensive sports car, they'll make a point out of pointing out the fresh leather scent of the car's interior, or ask them to "picture themselves" pulling up to their house in their new sports car. They'd use auto-suggestion by saying, "when you're in bed tonight, imagine how the neighbors look at you, see the pride in your spouse's eyes ..."

States of Emotion

☑ **Envy**
"Imagine yourself being the envy of all your friends!'"

☑ **Vanity**
"The gold in this necklace adds warmth and luster to your face, making everyone more beautiful!"

☑ **Practical**
"This item can be worn casually during the day, and can dress-up an outfit at night!"

☑ Added benefit

"Buy now and you will get this attractive gift completely free!"

☑ Easy and Effortless

"Just point and click to order and your shipment will arrive in three days."

Solid Investment

☑ "This reversible blouse can save you hundreds of dollars in clothing costs. Create dozens of new looks by pairing it with slacks, shorts, and skirts. It's made from 100% cotton and will never shrink or fade."

☑ Problem Solving

"Look slim and trim in this tummy tightening skirt. The secret panel makes you look as if you dropped ten pounds overnight!"

Summary

File this in the shocking, but true, category. When you are on TV or radio, your "selling words" are important, but it's also the commanding, confident way in which you say them.

Citing an example from above, if you are a car sales person and ask your potential buyer to "inhale the rich leather scent," you better ask this with absolute confidence. Imagine how you would feel if you detected a quiver in your sales person's voice? It would be as if they did not believe in their product, and were trying to pull a fast one on you.

Rehearsal and practice will easily conquer any hesitation you feel about bold promotion.

Your Assignment

☑   Pretend that what you are promoting will be featured on an infomercial. List its benefits.

☑   List the details that make what you're promoting unique.

☑   Create an imaginary customer for your product or service, and hand sell this individual using emotional, selling words.

Chapter 9
Booking Yourself on Radio Shows

In this chapter you will learn:
- ☑ How to position yourself for radio interviews
- ☑ How to sell more product on the air
- ☑ How to find radio show producer contacts

Even though entrepreneurs and authors alike dream of appearing on top rated TV shows like Oprah, the truth is that radio, more than other media, generates immediate purchases and is much more accessible. More consumers buy products within one hour of hearing a radio commercial than within one hour of seeing a TV commercial.

Today's long drive times, especially when the most affluent consumers are on the road, make radio especially attractive. Think of how many stations you have tuned to your car alone, and then multiply that into cities all across the country.

Best of all, radio is an effortless endeavor. Once you create your talking points, hook, and magnet messages, all you have to do is wake up and answer the phone and you're getting free media attention!

Simply conduct an interview from home on a clear telephone line. You don't need special equipment, just a bright voice and cheerful attitude. I would recommend a quiet atmosphere and disabling your call waiting while you conduct the interview.

Because literally thousands of radio stations would be thrilled to feature you if you position yourself appropriately, you'll have to take the added step of qualifying the show. Ask yourself these questions:

- ☑ Does the show reach your target audience?
- ☑ Does the show reach a large enough audience?
- ☑ Is the show "live?"

It may not be necessary to spend money sending a full press kit to the station or time writing a targeted pitch letter to a specific show, unless you're trying for a specific top-rated radio show with real name and promotion appeal.

Instead, begin by generating two or three versions of a pitch letter to fit specific show types, but always take care to personalize it with the name of the current producer or host.

Fax the letter, and don't forget the most important step of following up! If you went to the trouble of reading about the show in one of the media directories, you already know you're a good fit, so don't give up!

Giving interviews to radio stations has enormous benefits, including:

1. You can promote daily, reinforcing your message or product without jeopardizing your day job;
2. If you are self-employed, you won't have to take valuable time away from existing clients;
3. You don't necessarily have to leave the house;
4. You will quickly become so proficient you can do it in your sleep!

5. Most radio shows don't mind if you give out your toll-free number. In fact, the general rule is to reintroduce you every time the show returns from a commercial break. It doesn't hurt to provide with several different ways to introduce you;

6. There's much more time for chat on radio as opposed to TV, so you have more time to charm an audience into buying what you are promoting.

7. Since youwon't be customizing, you will quickly get your "script" down flat.

Live or Phone-Ins?

Gregory Godek, the besting author of the *1,001 Ways To Be Romantic* book/speaking franchise, swears by the promotional power of radio. He makes it his goal to conduct at least five phone-in shows a day as soon as he wakes from the convenience of his own home.

Telephone Interviews are easy, but it's fun to go to the station if you live nearby. The advantages to going to the station are these:

- ☑ It will make you feel like a star;
- ☑ You can personally give the operator your contact information so when viewers call after the show, he or she will direct them (and their dollars) to you;
- ☑ It will give you the opportunity to bond and connect with the host, station personnel, and the general manager. This is important because:

☑ You will want to let them know about a new project so you will be invited to appear again;

☑ You can query them for other show contacts so you can appear on them;

☑ You can ask for an endorsement (keep a file of these for future use);

☑ You can have a picture taken and with their permission, put it on your web site or use it for promotional purposes.

Radio has tremendous advantages.. Rehearse your magnet messages and you'll do just fine on "phoner" shows. Radio is similar to having a casual conversation over coffee with a million plus eavesdroppers joining in.

Which brings me to the main point of this chapter.

How To Position Yourself For an Effective Radio Interview

First off, relax! All the hard work is over! You snagged the interview and you are on a bullet train toward success!

If you've been reading this book in sequential order, than you already sent the producer your media kit, pitch letter, and related material. However, if you skipped right to this chapter, or received a media call out of the blue because you had your holiday listed in a book or they found out about you in a guest directory, you must send them material immediately.

Materials the Station Needs For an Effective Interview

☑ All your contact information, including email and web sites.

☑ Your toll free number.

☑ Your book, product, or material supporting the issue you are going to discuss on-air;

☑ List of questions for the host to ask you (note: don't be surprised if they haven't read the book or researched your product or service). Do this in a variety of ways for each return from commercial breaks;

☑ Scripted introduction (*write* how you want to be introduced, word for word! Don't leave something this important to chance)

Your Magic "One-Sheet"

This is a two-sided document you will create that will serve a variety of purposes, though it's primarily a "cheat sheet" for both you and the radio host. It's a document that can be sent via:

☑ Mail

☑ Fax

☑ Email

☑ Download from Web

The purpose of the Magic Sheet is to:

☑ Contain contact information on you;

☑ Position and reinforce your expert status, and let the host know who s/he is reckoning with;

116

- ☑ Reveal updates about your new books, articles, awards;

- ☑ Provide a scripted introduction;

- ☑ On its reverse side, explain your subject and why it's of benefit to the station's audience.

Don't be afraid to brag! Go into the interview with all guns blazing! Create lists of the following:

- ☑ Articles by you

- ☑ Articles about you

- ☑ Other media appearances

- ☑ Your recent books

- ☑ News about you or your company

- ☑ Recent awards

In tone and/or words, don't forget to allude to what a great value you will be to the audience! You can include snippets of good things other hosts or your audience had to say about you.

On the reverse side, you will want to freshen the host or producer's memory by recanting similar material you already shared in the pitch letter and media kit that got you booked. This may include:

- ☑ Why the subject you are speaking on is important;

- ☑ Why it needs to be acted upon NOW;

☑ Why it should be of interest to the station's listeners;

☑ Statistics, facts, anecdotes, and other supporting material.

How to Sell More Product on the Air

Every Media Magician has three tasks to accomplish on the air.

☑ Be of service to your audience by taking on an "expert's" roll and helping them solve an issue or improve their life with your advice;

☑ Telegraph the benefits of what you are promoting to compel them to buy, stressing how much the listener may risk losing or stand to gain by passing up the opportunity to buy into what you are selling NOW;

☑ How to contact you or where to buy your product.

Each of these benefits is important. We've all seen shrill guests on top-rated morning shows promoting themselves like used car salesmen. Be assertive and play the expert, but realize the "Jack and the Magic Beanstalk" effect and realize you are in the publicity game for the long haul.

A producer's worst fear is that you are going to turn the show into a non-stop commercial. They've been burnt before. The best thing you can do when you meet is shake their hand, look into their eyes, and say "I'm so thrilled you've invited me to speak to your audience. I really want to give you a great show!"

Other Great Tricks!

On radio it's important to have "shtick," a Hollywood word that can be roughly translated as "gimmick." Something to make you stand out from the crowd.

In radio land, what you want to do is create a "frenzy."

Make your segment fun and lively, and here are three ways to do just that.

- ☑ Contests;
- ☑ Quizzes;
- ☑ Free giveaway! This may include any of the below:
  - ebook (with ordering info for profitable book enclosed);
  - Booklet (with ordering info for profitable book enclosed);
  - Actual book, CD-rom, or other item of value available over the counter;
  - Tickets (to a seminar your giving or an event otherwise related to you and your product);
  - Coupon (discount, 2 for one)

So, how do you plan to structure your giveaways?

Creating a quiz or a contest is one of the strongest ways you can recoup sales profits.

How?

It reinforces your message, over and over again.

It gets people FOCUSED on your promotion.

Sly media magician that you are, you've got them hooked because everyone likes to win a prize.

The Quiz and Contest

The quest to win draws them to your contest and quiz. Once people realize that your product or book will help answer key questions they will turn to you.

It forces them to realize they may not know the answer, and thus realize the need for your book.

"You" Magic

Aren't you bored and tired with talk show guests who keep writing about the "proverbial I" which is themselves?

Listeners and viewers are too. First, let's give I-oriented guests the benefit of a doubt and accept that using the word "I" is perfectly legitimate in our society, and hardly brands them as an egomaniac.

But for a moment, consider your own listening habits. Wouldn't you rather see a product, book, or service from the standpoint of what it can offer you? The guest is really working the sales pitch to make a decent livelihood, but is that a reason why "we" should buy?

Strive to make your message "you oriented!"

Make use of "You Magic."

The Thirty Second Sound Bite

Do you know what thirty-seconds sounds like? No? I'll show you how to package your core message in thirty seconds, which is a good "earful" of time to answer a host's question.

Start by training yourself to understand how much talk it really takes to fill thirty seconds. Ask yourself questions you scripted (for the purpose of giving to the host beforehand) and answer them speaking into a tape recorder. Play it back. If you don't have a tape recorder, pretend you are the guest on talk radio shows you're listening to. When you hear the "live guest" answer the question, give an answer yourself. Does the host ask the next question before you are finished? If so, shorten your message.

How were you?

Be sure to use action words, emotional words, words that will motivate your prospect to buy!

Guarantee Friendly Phone Calls

Great! You booked yourself on a radio "phoner" (slang for a radio show which takes phone-in callers). You've practiced your Magnet Messages you are fully prepared. But are you really?

Now all you have to do is sit back and wait for the calls to roll in

The short answer is that you are not in control.

Listeners are like sheep and most wait for the first call-in to break the ice before they call in themselves.

Silent phones on radio is not a good thing!

Have a friend or relative phone in a question to get the show rolling. Your host will be happy, you will sound like the expert you are! But if you are going to the trouble to recruit a pal, give that pal clear instruction. In other words, neatly type out a script. You will want to include:

☑ A well-thought out question that encompasses at least one of your pre-meditated, pre-scripted message points (complete with facts, statistics, and example).

☑ Sound professional and ASK where to buy your book or product.

After the Phone-In Radio Show

The host will disconnect just after saying goodbye to you on air. Just hang up. If they want to contact you, they'll just call back.

1. Immediately, write a thank you note. Not only is this polite since the station has just given you a valuable promotional opportunity, but also because you have ulterior motives. In the note, say you'd love to be a "regular" guest speaking about your topic of expertise. This means that whenever they have a spot to fill, they'll call you to chat.

2. Ask the station for a testimonial (sometimes called a "blurb" or "endorsement) that you can use on your marketing material. Try drafting three examples yourself, and include any material that reinforces what you wrote about yourself (example: articles you've written, what others have said about you). It's good form to send a self addressed stamped envelope so they can return it to you easily.

Why Testimonials Are Important

Testimonials act as third party validation. They are extremely valuable to have and you never know when you might need one. A host can't say no to you if you don't ask.

The simpler you make the letter, the better. You might say, "I really enjoyed being on the show and worked to give a great performance. If you feel any of these three statements describes a statement you might make about me, can you circle it and send it back in the enclosed envelope? Keep the accolade short and simple. Write a single sentence you think someone you just met would feel comfortable saying about you, something like "Sarah Smarts was great on the air!" or something short, fun, and informative describing you as a guest.

Keep In Contact

Create a media database with the kind of contact software that will allow you to touch base with them at least twice a year with updates about you and your product.

Summary:

Radio is the easiest, most effective form of advertising in today's competitive media world. Even better, it's free. The secret of selling your products, books, or services on air is to present yourself as an expert authority on your subject.

As best-selling author Greg Godek suggested, it's crucial that you make a daily goal of how many "phoners" you wish to do. Endear yourself to the radio stations and do your best to market yourself as the kind of guest they can call any time for answers about the subject of your expertise.

Create information folders for your radio appearances, so that you can grab a folder and sound confident on your subject in an instant. Have a tip sheet handy so that you can enumerate points. And, as always, have a headset so that you can converse in comfort.

Media Magic

Remember after every interview to send a thank you note, not email to the producer. Include a little "something extra" such as a signed photo of yourself, book, or small inexpensive (under $1) gift that somehow reflects your topic of expertise. Example: If you wrote a book on collecting classic cars, what about sending a toy car and appreciative note? You can even send message pads with your photo/contact information on them. This also reminds them that when they need a guest, you're available.

☑ Dedicate an hour this very day to creating some or all of the documents that will comprise your radio show folder, such as your tip sheet.

☑ Send a friend a list of questions and arrange for them to call you for a "phone interview." If you can arrange it, tape yourself. Replay the tape and rate your performance. Note areas of improvement and practice until perfect.

Assignment:

☑ Consider creating thank you notes specific to your appearances on TV and Radio shows, i.e. with your logo and contact information on it.

☑ Brainstorm an inexpensive, appropriate gift to send.

Chapter 10
Booking Yourself on Television

In this chapter you will learn:
☑   How to go from local to national TV
☑   How to profit from being a great guest
☑   Tips for successful appearances

It's natural to want to make an appearance on the top TV shows, but when you're first starting out, you'll be grateful for the opportunity to work your way toward the top.

First, you'll be getting some much needed on-air practice. And second, you'll be in the position to have tape on yourself so you can send it to bigger shows when they ask for it.

If you can't afford a media trainer, you'll do well to invest in a portable video camera and practice either alone, or with a friend interviewing you on tape. Don't be overly critical as you review your performance, but do strive to take note of your weaknesses and turn them into strengths.

Once you have rehearsed your talking points, magnet messages, and the facts, statistics, and anecdotes that will support the above, you are ready to be on the air!

I strongly advise starting with your local community cable station. Chances are that if you subscribe to cable stations you've seen a local TV production. In their agreement with the city they broadcast in, cable companies have to agree to put a certain amount of money and a channel aside for use by the community.

Every community has one, from Los Angeles to New York, allowing members of the community to reach millions of viewers each week. Booking yourself on one of these shows will give you several benefits:

- ☑ You will have a taped interview of yourself to send national producers who request it;
- ☑ When surfing stations, your colleagues will see your appearance;
- ☑ You can use your appearance as the basis of a press release;
- ☑ You can send the tape to other community TV stations across the country for airing;
- ☑ It provides excellent training for when you are booked on a national show;
- ☑ You can practice many of the techniques you will learn in this book on a smaller stage.

In short, getting on local TV and radio is the best way to gradually warm up to the idea of being live on the airwaves and

Step One – Dialing for Digits

Your first step is to call the Alliance for Community Media at (202) 393-2650 and ask them for the phone numbers for community access stations in your area.

They, more than your local library, would be up to date about public resources in your community. You can also order a directory of public access stations for your own use.

While your chances of getting booked as a guest on a community public access TV show are higher (and can happen faster) than on a national daytime television show, you will still have to put together an impressive pitch letter (or fax) and be prepared to give "good telephone."

Making the Call

Begin by calling the station, and in your most pleasant and friendly voice, chat up whoever answers the phone. At many stations, whomever answers the phone has the skinny on what's going on at the station and which producer will best serve your needs.

Your objective is to find a match between what you want to promote (though you won't phrase it this way!) and a producer who covers your area.

Tying In With The Community

The correct way to phrase it is that you are a resident of the community and want to help/inform other residents by talking about "xyz" on the air.

Offer Expert Tips!

If you are a tax accountant, you can offer tips on helping residents lower their taxes, or if you've written a cookbook featuring Italian cooking, explain that you want to explain the heart-healthy benefits of Italian cooking to your community.

Getting Past the Gatekeeper

The person who answers the phone is, of course, only the gatekeeper. He or she will ideally give you the name and contact information of the producer best suited to your area.

Try calling first, because public access is lower key than national TV. Explain who you are, your credentials, and how you want to help them put on a great show. Offer to fax or send information immediately.

It's important to be as polite and professional as possible because of the wide assortment of personalities you will encounter. To you, there may be a world of difference between appearing on Larry King and appearing on a TV show that only is seen by 30,000 people. But the producer and talk show host at a community station feel themselves to be equal to Larry King.

If, for whatever reason, the producer does not feel you are a good fit for the show, ask if they can recommend another producer. People are very helpful at community stations and will assist you if they can.

In addition, you can also send a flier advertising yourself as a potential guest to the public access station itself. While faxing is a fast way to do this, a colorful, eye-attracting flier is best sent through the mail. You may want to score the bottom of the flier with stubs that have your name and number written on them, so producers can tear them off and call you.

Making the Personal Connection

You want to make a personal connection with the staff and the producers at your community station, so make an effort to watch the channels and see what shows might be a good fit for you. The staff can be extremely helpful in matching you up with an otherwise elusive producer, so I'd go the extra mile and would put a lot of energy into motivating them to want to help you. Visiting the station is an excellent first step.

Remember, the objective isn't just to get seen by 30,000 people in your community. It's to get yourself on tape to send to potentially bigger fish down the line.

Choosing a Slant

Giving a pitch letter a slant for community television follows the same principles for other TV and radio shows. This book details many innovative approaches, but since you are in a crunch for time, I'm listing a few again for your convenience:

1. Piggyback on local news. This is an especially powerful slant for a community television station. Position yourself in your pitch letter as someone who can answer the community's questions or benefit them in some way;

2. Look up a holiday in Chase's Book of Days or John Kremer's Celebrate Today and create an association between them.

Follow Up

Follow up with the station or the producers until you get an airdate, which should be at least a few weeks away. Until then, continue on with this daily program and you will learn the tricks of being great on the air!

From Local Community to City to National

Once you're on the air you'll discover that publicity begets more publicity! Send footage of yourself on the community show to your local morning show with a targeted pitch letter, again careful to tie what you're promoting to the community.

Then, send the tapes you've made of yourself being interviewed on your local channels to national shows, using the tactics we discussed when covering the targeted pitch letter.

Other Ways to Capitalize On Your Media Performances

☑ Stamp "as seen on television!" on your promotional material;

☑ Have a picture taken of you with the host, write a clever caption, and send it to the print media;

☑ Add the show to your "media appearance" list;

☑ Use appearance to lure bigger shows!

Practice Really Does Make Perfect!

Mark Twain reportedly said it takes three weeks to prepare a good ad-lib speech. Start preparing for your TV interview today.

Your success hinges on three elements:

1. Preparation
2. Content
3. Delivery

Once you've developed your Magnet Messages, you will want to practice by having a friend "play host" and read them to you. Answer the questions using the Magnet Messages as the core, always offering facts and statistics and even anecdotes you've already developed to support your position.

Another good tactic is to inject your responses with as much color and enthusiasm as you can muster, striving to relate them with a story currently playing itself out in the news, if possible. You want to use forceful words and an active voice. Deliver the "meat" of your argument at the beginning; don't wait for a later opportunity that may never materialize. Show the goods right away!

Keep your voice upbeat and energetic, unless the topic makes this an impossible option. Also use examples and personal stories to underscore how what your promoting will make the audience happier, more successful, experience greater ease, and fulfilled.

Create transition statements in case the host asks a silly question or one that you might prefer not to answer.

Finally, as backup, you may want to consider adding three to six additional points. Sometimes other guests fail to show or the host finds you more interesting. If you are asked to speak longer, you will need more relevant content.

Write Out Your Introduction In Advance

An introduction whets the audience's appetite for what is to come next. Between commercial breaks, savvy

Media Magic

TV and radio stations script introductions that are really "teasers" to use industry jargon. Teasers promote what will come next in a powerful way. In short, it makes the audience feel that if they don't return, they'll be missing something really important and educational.

Dale Carnegie, a best-selling author and motivational speaker, outlines the elements necessary for a successful introduction. They include:

☑ The individual's credentials & education;

☑ Their company and title;

☑ Why what they say is timely;

☑ How you can benefit by listening closely to them.

According to Carnegie, the most important element is the enthusiasm the host intones as s/he introduces you.

The level of enthusiasm used in your introduction you have no control over. But, take initiative by scripting your own introduction, and I'll wager it will be read 100% as you scripted it. Your television appearance is too important to leave to chance.

Sorting out the Programming

☑ **Local News Programs**
- Thrive on diversity in their broadcast, including national and local news.

☑   **News Shows**

- National shows such as 60 Minutes, 20/
  20, Dateline. These feature longer
  segments and focus on trends. When you
  pitch to these shows, be sure to "create
  your show" in the sense that you will add
  other potential guests to be featured in the
  segment to show balance not just self-
  promotion.

☑ **Talk Shows**

- Your best bet! Again, watch the shows
  and determine your perfect fit.

Pump yourself up! Energize! Don't just "think"
you'll be great. Vividly see yourself being great in your
mind's eye! Create a movie of how wonderful you'll be
and play it over and over in your mind.

The truth is, the audience audience really wants to
see you enjoying yourself and at ease.

Arrive at the Station Early!

Any time you make a media appearance, it's a
good idea to arrive early. You will get the lay of the land,
and prompt arrival will give you a moment to privately
review your message points.

What to Wear

Dress conventionally (assuming this is your
platform) but also try to "image brand." Chefs, for
example, might wear a toque. At the same time, dress in
a way that flatters. Ladies, just a few key words of advice.
First, though black is a fashionable color, consider how

severe it might look for a cheerful, upbeat morning show. (hint: a peach suit is ideal). Second, if you do wear a shorter skirt, practice sitting in front of the mirror. And finally, if you do wear jewelry make sure it won't make noise or clang against the microphone.

Men should wear a suit, a tie, and polished shoes if they want to come across as authoritative. Realize that the audience is constantly searching for visual clues about a guest outside what they say, so make sure your dress supports your message.

The Interview Starts the Moment You Enter the Station

TV producers and hosts size you up the moment you enter the station. Walk tall and speak with confidence. Realize that ninety percent of communication is non-verbal, so you communicate your message without saying a word.

When you are "on air" be commanding but polite. Remember that the audience is on the side of the host, not you. They welcome this host into their homes every day and you are a stranger. It's surprising how often guests are rude to their hosts.

Try to develop a good on-air banter with the host as if you're "co-host," working together with the host to make the show fun, enlightening, and a success.

When you are introduced to the producer and/or host, shake their hand with confidence, look them in the eye, smile and tell them you are there to give them a great show.

Where to Look

Look at your host because you don't know which camera will be focused on you. If you are very sure of yourself and want to make a point, it is okay to look directly at the camera — but just do this once. Hosts dislike it as it feels as if you are upstaging them.

Body Language

Be commanding and forceful in your posture. If you make a gesture, make it bold. Be comfortable, but not too comfortable.

Contact Information

Ask the producer or host if it would be okay to give out your toll free number or web site at the end of the show. Also confirm the spelling of your name used as an on screen identifier.

After The Show

After the show, if there's time chat up the host. See if you can brainstorm an intriguing way into being invited back. Steel yourself because you should also ask two questions guests are reluctant to ask, but questions that are usually affirmatively answered.

☑ "I enjoyed the show. Is it possible for you to give me an endorsement?"

☑ "This was fun! Do you have any other friends in the media who might enjoy interviewing me?"

☑ A thank you note will be most appreciated!

Summary:

The key to a successful television interview is practice, practice, practice. You must come across well-rehearsed, an expert, and likable. Start with the local media, build a reputation as a great guest, and go national.

Realize that talk show hosts speak with each other and that word of your being a great guet gets around.

Your Assignment:

☑   Watch at least five talk show hosts a day and make notes of what guests that worked well in your opinion, and what didn't work at all.

☑   If you're not a "smiler," begin to learn how to smile now! A smile sends a subconscious message to the audience implying that you're trustworthy and likable.

☑   If you do video tape yourself, look out for areas of improvement, but at the same time, congratulate yourself for what you did right!

Chapter 11
Why You (Yes, You!) Can Profit and Promote on TV and Radio!

In this chapter you'll learn:

☑ Why self-belief is crucial in media success

☑ How to create affirmations

☑ Tapping into the magic of our subconscious minds

For a moment, think back on your greatest moments of triumph and achievement. This moment may be when you:

☑ Established a new business;

☑ Completed a book;

☑ Created a product;

You of all people know that this triumph didn't happen by *accident* or even overnight! You spent a lot of mental energy putting yourself in the right place at the right time, sowing the right seeds, and effort into making it happen.

Visualization is Key

Leading reports from brain researchers site cybernetic studies showing that our minds cannot differentiate between a real and an imaginary experience. The sooner we "train our brain" to see and visualize ourselves appearing with ease on the media circuit, the more quickly it will manifest into reality.

See Yourself Achieve Your Goals

The mind is a powerful tool that operates best on a visual plane. To fully understand this power of suggestion think of dining on tender spring lamb with tart cherry sauce. You don't see the words, you see the image. You might even feel a tart pucker in your mouth, or sense the tenderness of the lamb.

In the same way, the mind sees all events, whether they're past, present, future, or imaginary, as an *image*. Conditioning your mind to visualize your business or product thriving as a result of your media efforts is one of the key components of this book. The more energy you put into visualization the faster it will become true for you.

Media attention is great for the ego, but the publicity must serve a larger, more direct purpose. *What you ask?* Positive publicity will attract more customers and motivate people to buy your book or product? This is the desired "end goal" you will achieve as a result of media publicity. Getting on *Oprah* may be your media goal, but if your appearance on the show does not help promote you or your product to a target audience, then there isn't much point.

Write down a simple declaration of what you want to happen as a result of your media appearance. Example: I want to sell "x" books or products or receive "x" calls from potential new clients.

Once written, close your eyes, relax, and let your creative imagination paint a picture of yourself in the "after" scenario. Visualize yourself in your office or wherever it is that you do your work, and see yourself surrounded by the manifestations of your media success.

You could be checking with your distributor and seeing the huge increase in orders for your books. You could visualize yourself walking into the office and seeing your assistant try to handle the many calls coming in, wanting your help with their business. You can see product orders skyrocket.

Whatever it is, visualize this image clearly and internalize it!

Make it a practice to *see* this image, for at lest five seconds, five times a day. Let it fill you with pride and satisfaction.

Now that you've set and seen your visualized goal, you will begin the process of creating positive affirmations.

Positive Affirmations

Positive affirmations serve to build body and soul by canceling any negativity or insecurity about your talent or goals.

Everyone, even big stars, often become apprehensive before a show date. But the best of them have mastered the art of using positive affirmations to put themselves at ease.

The basic premise is to give yourself positive messages.

Messages Can Be

☑ Performed silently
☑ Spoken aloud
☑ Written down
Ideally, a combination of all three.

Media Magic

Keep a steady stream of positive affirmations running through your mind at all times.

Benefiting From Your Positive Affirmations
1. Always phrase affirmations in the present tense (as if what you desire already exists);
2. Phrase affirmations in an enthusiastic way;
3. Short, direct affirmations are the most effective.

Shakti Gawain, author of the book *Creative Visualization,* recommends that you take an affirmation and write it ten to twenty times on a piece of paper using your name in the first, second, and third person.

Examples:

☑ I, Eddie Entrepreneur, am accomplishing my daily goals;

☑ Eddie, you are accomplishing your daily goals in your *Magic Book*;

☑ Eddie Entrepreneur has now accomplished his daily goals in his *Magic Book*.

Even if you don't really believe affirmations will get you anywhere, but manage to speak and say the affirmations as if you did, you will see your affirmations come to reality.

Banishing Mind-Yapping

What is mind yapping? Allowing negativity and self doubt to interfere with your success.

Me? Why should I sabotage myself?
Psychologists have considered several reasons:
1. Success is a responsibility;

Marisa D'Vari

2. You want your life to dramatically change, yet you are afraid of change;

3. Becoming a success will change the direction of your life forever, and you are not sure you want it changed. Secretly, you fear you can't measure up;

   Combat mind yapping by refusing to acknowledge a negative thought – ever!

Endnotes

Becoming a regular guest for TV and radio shows is much easier than you think!

I'm constantly adding media release forms and other key information to my site, so I encourage you to check in at http://www.GetBookedNow.com often.

I also offer a free, weekly ezine that focuses on how you can get free publicity and includes updates of these publicity-savvy forms you can copy for your own use. Join at the http://www.deg.com main page.

I created this book to help you brainstorm your own media success, and would love to hear your comments at mdvari@deg.com

The world needs the information you have to offer!

Wishing you much magic!

Resources

Getting TV/Radio Producers to Call You

Radio-TV Interview Reports
800 989 1400x713
Bradley Communications

Yearbook of Experts, Authorities, & Spokespersons
Broadcast Interview Source, Inc.
800 932 7266

Organizations Helpful for Writers, Entrepreneurs, & Self-Promoters

Publisher's Marketing Association (PMA)
310-372-2732
http://www.PMA-online.org

Small Publisher's Association of North America (SPAN)   719-395-4790
http://www.spannet.org

National Speakers Associations (NSA)
480-968-2552
http://www.nsaspeaker.org/

Writing, Publishing, Speaking, Motivational Books:

Breakthrough Intuition, by Rosemary Ellen Guiley, Berkley Pub Group.

1,001 Ways to Market Your Book, by John Kremer, Open Horizons.

Accidental Genius: Revolutionize Your Thinking Through Private Writing, by Mark Levy, Berrett-Koehler Pub.

The Self-Publishing Manual, by Dan Poynter, Para Publishing.

The Complete Guide to Self-Publishing, by Tom and Marilyn Ross, Writer's Digest Books.

Jump Start Your Book Sales, by Tom and Marilyn Ross, Writer's Digest Books.

Shameless Marketing for Brazen Hussies: 307 Awesome Money-Making Strategies for Savvy Entrepreneurs, by Marilyn Ross, Communication Creativity.

Speak and Grow Rich, by Dottie and Lilly Walters, Prentice Hall.

Helpful Web Sites!

Here you have access to hundreds of free articles, informative links, and tools that will enable you to succeed in your magical media endeavors.

Marisa D'Vari's Web Site
http://www.deg.com

Dan Poynter's Web Site
http://www.parapublishing.com

John Kremer's Web Sites
http://www.JohnKremer.com
http://www.celebratetoday.com

Publisher's Marketing Association (PMA)
http://www.pma-online.org

Mary Westheimer's Web Site
http://www.bookzone.com

Sam Horn
http://www.SamHorn.com

Angela Adair-Hoy's BookLocker Web Site
http://www.booklocker.com

Rosemary Guiley's Web Site
http://www.VisionaryLiving.com

Gregory Godek's Web Site
http://www.1001WaysToBeRomantic.com

John Fuhrman's Web Site
http://www.ExpertSpeak.com

Marcia Yudkin's Web Site
http://www.yudkin.com

Dan Seidman's Web Site
http://www.salesautopsy.com

National Speakers Association (NSA) Web Site
http://www.nsaspeaker.org

American Society of Journalists and Authors
http://www.asja.org

Jim Cox's MidWest Book Review Web Site
http://www.execpc.com/~mbr/bookwatch/

Mark Levy's Web Site
http://www.GeniusTown.com

Larry James
http://CelebrateLove.Com

Lisbeth Wiley Chapman
http://www.InkAir.com

Message from Marisa!

Dear Media Magician:

I really enjoyed sharing my media magic with you!
All too often, we read valuable material but neglect to
put it to immediate use!

To make sure you get all the media you can handle,
I've made special services available to you on my web
site, http://www.GetBookedNow.com

You can also benefit from my free ezine!
You will find a sign up box on any page on my
http://www.deg.com web site. Or send an email to
join-BusinessSuccessSolutions@pluto.sparklist.com

Wishing you much magic!

mdvari@deg.com